Collins Gem
FRENCH
Grammar

CollinsGem
An Imprint of HarperCollins*Publishers*

third edition 2001

© William Collins Sons & Co Ltd 1984
© HarperCollins Publishers 1994, 2001

latest reprint 2002

ISBN 0-00-710208-9

Collins Gem® is a registered trademark of
HarperCollins Publishers Limited

www.collins.co.uk

_____

The HarperCollins USA website address is
www.harpercollins.com

_____

Lesley A Robertson • Lorna Sinclair

editorial staff
Christine Penman, Megan Thomson

editorial management
Vivian Marr

_____

A catalogue record for this book is available
from the British Library

Typeset by Ruth Noble, Peebles

Printed and bound in Italy by Amadeus S.p.A.

INTRODUCTION

The **Collins Gem French Grammar** is designed to offer students of French of all ages and at all levels an uncluttered, step-by-step guide to the grammar of the language. For the person with little or no knowledge of French it provides the basic 'tools' necessary for comprehension and communication, and for the more advanced learner it provides an efficient and speedy means of reference and revision.

As you will see from the contents list overleaf, the book is split into sections according to part of speech (nouns, articles, adjectives etc) or grammar point (sentence structure, use of numbers etc). As far as is possible, we have tried to anticipate any grammatical terms with which you may not be familiar, and a brief explanation is given at the relevant point in the text.

A special feature of this book is the clear demarcation of grammatical points, each of which is treated on a left-hand page and illustrated by numerous practical, up-to-date examples on the opposite right-hand page. For instance, turn to page 154 and you will see a series of boxed numbers → ⒈ to → ⒑ throughout the text on that page. These numbers cross-refer you to an example, or group of examples, on page 155. This double-page layout gives you maximum accessibility to the grammar point you want to learn or revise, while the examples help fix that grammar point firmly in your mind.

Special attention is paid throughout the book to potential problem areas – such as sentence structure, where French usage can differ markedly from English usage. In addition, the section on translation problems alerts you to some of the most common pitfalls of translation. A full index, with both grammatical topics and key words in French and English, completes the grammar.

ABBREVIATIONS

ctd.	continued	**p(p)**	page(s)	**qn**	quelqu'un
fem.	feminine	**perf.**	perfect	**sb**	somebody
infin.	infinitive	**plur.**	plural	**sing.**	singular
masc.	masculine	**qch**	quelque chose	**sth**	something

CONTENTS

CONTENTS

Grammar

VERBS

❏ Simple Tenses: formation

In French the simple tenses are:

Present	→ ①
Imperfect	→ ②
Future	→ ③
Conditional	→ ④
Past Historic	→ ⑤
Present Subjunctive	→ ⑥
Imperfect Subjunctive	→ ⑦

They are formed by adding endings to a verb stem. The endings show the number and person of the subject of the verb → ⑧

The stem and endings of regular verbs are totally predictable. The following sections show all the patterns for regular verbs. For irregular verbs see pp 74 ff.

❏ Regular Verbs

There are three regular verb patterns (called conjugations), each identifiable by the ending of the infinitive:

- First conjugation verbs end in **-er** e.g. **donner** to give
- Second conjugation verbs end in **-ir** e.g. **finir** to finish
- Third conjugation verbs end in **-re** e.g. **vendre** to sell

These three conjugations are treated in order on the following pages.

1	**je donne**	I give I am giving I do give
2	**je donnais**	I gave I was giving I used to give
3	**je donnerai**	I shall give I shall be giving
4	**je donnerais**	I should/would give I should/would be giving
5	**je donnai**	I gave
6	**(que) je donne**	(that) I give/gave
7	**(que) je donnasse**	(that) I gave
8	**je donne** **nous donnons** **je donnerais** **nous donnerions**	I give we give I would give we would give

☐ Simple Tenses: First Conjugation

• The stem is formed as follows:

TENSE	FORMATION	EXAMPLE
Present Imperfect Past Historic Present Subjunctive Imperfect Subjunctive	infinitive minus **-er**	**donn-**
Future Conditional	infinitive	**donner-**

• To the appropriate stem add the following endings:

		PRESENT → 1	IMPERFECT → 2	PAST HISTORIC → 3
	1st person	**-e**	**-ais**	**-ai**
sing.	2nd person	**-es**	**-ais**	**-as**
	3rd person	**-e**	**-ait**	**-a**
	1st person	**-ons**	**-ions**	**-âmes**
plur.	2nd person	**-ez**	**-iez**	**-âtes**
	3rd person	**-ent**	**-aient**	**-èrent**

		PRESENT SUBJUNCTIVE → 4	IMPERFECT SUBJUNCTIVE → 5
	1st person	**-e**	**-asse**
sing.	2nd person	**-es**	**-asses**
	3rd person	**-e**	**-ât**
	1st person	**-ions**	**-assions**
plur.	2nd person	**-iez**	**-assiez**
	3rd person	**-ent**	**-assent**

		FUTURE → 6	CONDITIONAL → 7
	1st person	**-ai**	**-ais**
sing.	2nd person	**-as**	**-ais**
	3rd person	**-a**	**-ait**
	1st person	**-ons**	**-ions**
plur.	2nd person	**-ez**	**-iez**
	3rd person	**-ont**	**-aient**

1 PRESENT	2 IMPERFECT	3 PAST HISTORIC
je donne	je donnais	je donnai
tu donnes	tu donnais	tu donnas
il donne	il donnait	il donna
elle donne	elle donnait	elle donna
nous donnons	nous donnions	nous donnâmes
vous donnez	vous donniez	vous donnâtes
ils donnent	ils donnaient	ils donnèrent
elles donnent	elles donnaient	elles donnèrent

4 PRESENT SUBJUNCTIVE	5 IMPERFECT SUBJUNCTIVE
je donne	je donnasse
tu donnes	tu donnasses
il donne	il donnât
elle donne	elle donnât
nous donnions	nous donnassions
vous donniez	vous donnassiez
ils donnent	ils donnassent
elles donnent	elles donnassent

6 FUTURE	7 CONDITIONAL
je donnerai	je donnerais
tu donneras	tu donnerais
il donnera	il donnerait
elle donnera	elle donnerait
nous donnerons	nous donnerions
vous donnerez	vous donneriez
ils donneront	ils donneraient
elles donneront	elles donneraient

◻ Simple Tenses: Second Conjugation

+ The stem is formed as follows:

TENSE	FORMATION	EXAMPLE
Present		
Imperfect		
Past Historic	infinitive minus -ir	fin-
Present Subjunctive		
Imperfect Subjunctive		
Future	infinitive	finir-
Conditional		

+ To the appropriate stem add the following endings:

		PRESENT → ①	IMPERFECT → ②	PAST HISTORIC → ③
	1st person	-is	-issais	-is
sing.	2nd person	-is	-issais	-is
	3rd person	-it	-issait	-it
	1st person	-issons	-issions	-îmes
plur.	2nd person	-issez	-issiez	-îtes
	3rd person	-issent	-issaient	-irent

		PRESENT SUBJUNCTIVE → ④	IMPERFECT SUBJUNCTIVE → ⑤
	1st person	-isse	-isse
sing.	2nd person	-isses	-isses
	3rd person	-isse	-ît
	1st person	-issions	-issions
plur.	2nd person	-issiez	-issiez
	3rd person	-issent	-issent

		FUTURE → ⑥	CONDITIONAL → ⑦
	1st person	-ai	-ais
sing.	2nd person	-as	-ais
	3rd person	-a	-ait
	1st person	-ons	-ions
plur.	2nd person	-ez	-iez
	3rd person	-ont	-aient

	1 PRESENT		2 IMPERFECT		3 PAST HISTORIC
je	finis	je	finissais	je	finis
tu	finis	tu	finissais	tu	finis
il	finit	il	finissait	il	finit
elle	finit	elle	finissait	elle	finit
nous	finissons	nous	finissions	nous	finîmes
vous	finissez	vous	finissiez	vous	finîtes
ils	finissent	ils	finissaient	ils	finirent
elles	finissent	elles	finissaient	elles	finirent

	4 PRESENT SUBJUNCTIVE		5 IMPERFECT SUBJUNCTIVE
je	finisse	je	finisse
tu	finisses	tu	finisses
il	finisse	il	finît
elle	finisse	elle	finît
nous	finissions	nous	finissions
vous	finissiez	vous	finissiez
ils	finissent	ils	finissent
elles	finissent	elles	finissent

	6 FUTURE		7 CONDITIONAL
je	finirai	je	finirais
tu	finiras	tu	finirais
il	finira	il	finirait
elle	finira	elle	finirait
nous	finirons	nous	finirions
vous	finirez	vous	finiriez
ils	finiront	ils	finiraient
elles	finiront	elles	finiraient

◻ Simple Tenses: Third Conjugation

- The stem is formed as follows:

TENSE	FORMATION	EXAMPLE
Present Imperfect Past Historic Present Subjunctive Imperfect Subjunctive	infinitive minus -re	vend-
Future Conditional	infinitive minus -e	vendr-

- To the appropriate stem add the following endings:

		PRESENT → 1	IMPERFECT → 2	PAST HISTORIC → 3
sing.	1st person	-s	-ais	-is
	2nd person	-s	-ais	-is
	3rd person	–	-ait	-it
plur.	1st person	-ons	-ions	-îmes
	2nd person	-ez	-iez	-îtes
	3rd person	-ent	-aient	-irent

		PRESENT SUBJUNCTIVE → 4	IMPERFECT SUBJUNCTIVE → 5
sing.	1st person	-e	-isse
	2nd person	-es	-isses
	3rd person	-e	-ît
plur.	1st person	-ions	-issions
	2nd person	-iez	-issiez
	3rd person	-ent	-issent

		FUTURE → 6	CONDITIONAL → 7
sing.	1st person	-ai	-ais
	2nd person	-as	-ais
	3rd person	-a	-ait
plur.	1st person	-ons	-ions
	2nd person	-ez	-iez
	3rd person	-ont	-aient

1 PRESENT		2 IMPERFECT		3 PAST HISTORIC	
je	vend**s**	je	vend**ais**	je	vend**is**
tu	vend**s**	tu	vend**ais**	tu	vend**is**
il	vend	il	vend**ait**	il	vend**it**
elle	vend	elle	vend**ait**	elle	vend**it**
nous	vend**ons**	nous	vend**ions**	nous	vend**îmes**
vous	vend**ez**	vous	vend**iez**	vous	vend**îtes**
ils	vend**ent**	ils	vend**aient**	ils	vend**irent**
elles	vend**ent**	elles	vend**aient**	elles	vend**irent**

4 PRESENT SUBJUNCTIVE		5 IMPERFECT SUBJUNCTIVE	
je	vend**e**	je	vend**isse**
tu	vend**es**	tu	vend**isses**
il	vend**e**	il	vend**ît**
elle	vend**e**	elle	vend**ît**
nous	vend**ions**	nous	vend**issions**
vous	vend**iez**	vous	vend**issiez**
ils	vend**ent**	ils	vend**issent**
elles	vend**ent**	elles	vend**issent**

6 FUTURE		7 CONDITIONAL	
je	vend**rai**	je	vend**rais**
tu	vend**ras**	tu	vend**rais**
il	vend**ra**	il	vend**rait**
elle	vend**ra**	elle	vend**rait**
nous	vend**rons**	nous	vend**rions**
vous	vend**rez**	vous	vend**riez**
ils	vend**ront**	ils	vend**raient**
elles	vend**ront**	elles	vend**raient**

◻ First Conjugation Spelling Irregularities

Before certain endings, the stems of some '**-er**' verbs may change slightly.

Below, and on subsequent pages, the verb types are identified, and the changes described are illustrated by means of a representative verb.

Verbs ending: **-cer**
Change: **c** becomes **ç** before **a** or **o**
Tenses affected: Present, Imperfect, Past Historic, Imperfect
    Subjunctive, Present Participle
Model: **lancer** *to throw* → 1

- Why the change occurs:
  A cedilla is added to the **c** to retain its soft [s] pronunciation before the vowels **a** and **o**.

Verbs ending: **-ger**
Change: **g** becomes **ge** before **a** or **o**
Tenses affected: Present, Imperfect, Past Historic, Imperfect
    Subjunctive, Present Participle
Model: **manger** *to eat* → 2

- Why the change occurs:
  An **e** is added after the **g** to retain its soft [ʒ] pronunciation before the vowels **a** and **o**.

① INFINITIVE	PRESENT PARTICIPLE
lancer	**lançant**

PRESENT		IMPERFECT	
je	lance	je	**lançais**
tu	lances	tu	**lançais**
il/elle	lance	**il/elle**	**lançait**
nous	**lançons**	nous	lancions
vous	lancez	vous	lanciez
ils/elles	lancent	**ils/elles**	**lançaient**

PAST HISTORIC		IMPERFECT SUBJUNCTIVE	
je	**lançai**	je	**lançasse**
tu	**lanças**	tu	**lançasses**
il/elle	**lança**	**il/elle**	**lançât**
nous	**lançâmes**	**nous**	**lançassions**
vous	**lançâtes**	**vous**	**lançassiez**
ils/elles	lancèrent	**ils/elles**	**lançassent**

② INFINITIVE	PRESENT PARTICIPLE
manger	**mangeant**

PRESENT		IMPERFECT	
je	mange	**je**	**mangeais**
tu	manges	**tu**	**mangeais**
il/elle	mange	**il/elle**	**mangeait**
nous	**mangeons**	nous	mangions
vous	mangez	vous	mangiez
ils/elles	mangent	**ils/elles**	**mangeaient**

PAST HISTORIC		IMPERFECT SUBJUNCTIVE	
je	**mangeai**	**je**	**mangeasse**
tu	**mangeas**	**tu**	**mangeasses**
il/elle	**mangea**	**il/elle**	**mangeât**
nous	**mangeâmes**	**nous**	**mangeassions**
vous	**mangeâtes**	**vous**	**mangeassiez**
ils/elles	mangèrent	**ils/elles**	**mangeassent**

◻ First Conjugation Spelling Irregularities *(Continued)*

Verbs ending : **-eler**
Change: **-l** doubles before **-e**, **-es**, **-ent** and throughout the Future and Conditional tenses
Tenses affected: Present, Present Subjunctive, Future, Conditional
Model: **appeler** *to call* → ⬚1

- EXCEPTIONS: **geler** *to freeze* } like **mener** (p 18)
  peler *to peel*

Verbs ending : **-eter**
Change: **-t** doubles before **-e**, **-es**, **-ent** and throughout the Future and Conditional tenses
Tenses affected: Present, Present Subjunctive, Future, Conditional
Model: **jeter** *to throw* → ⬚2

- EXCEPTIONS: **acheter** *to buy* } like **mener** (p 18)
  haleter *to pant*

Verbs ending : **-yer**
Change: **y** changes to **i** before **-e**, **-es**, **-ent** and throughout the Future and Conditional tenses
Tenses affected: Present, Present Subjunctive, Future, Conditional
Model: **essuyer** *to wipe* → ⬚3

- The change described is optional for verbs ending in **-ayer** e.g. **payer** *to pay*, **essayer** *to try*.

Examples

1

	PRESENT (+ SUBJUNCTIVE)	FUTURE	
	j'appelle		j'appellerai
tu	appelles	tu	appelleras
il/elle	appelle	il	appellera *etc*
nous	appelons		
	(appelions)		CONDITIONAL
vous	appelez		j'appellerais
	(appeliez)	tu	appellerais
ils/elles	appellent	il	appellerait *etc*

2

	PRESENT (+ SUBJUNCTIVE)	FUTURE	
je	jette	je	jetterai
tu	jettes	tu	jetteras
il/elle	jette	il	jettera *etc*
nous	jetons		
	(jetions)		CONDITIONAL
vous	jetez	je	jetterais
	(jetiez)	tu	jetterais
ils/elles	jettent	il	jetterait *etc*

3

	PRESENT (+ SUBJUNCTIVE)	FUTURE	
	j'essuie		j'essuierai
tu	essuies	tu	essuieras
il/elle	essuie	il	essuiera *etc*
nous	essuyons		
	(essuyions)		CONDITIONAL
vous	essuyez		j'essuierais
	(essuyiez)	tu	essuierais
ils/elles	essuient	il	essuierait *etc*

◻ First Conjugation Spelling Irregularities *(Continued)*

Verbs ending	**mener, peser, lever** *etc*
Change:	**e** changes to **è**, before **-e, -es, -ent** and throughout the Future and Conditional tenses
Tenses affected:	Present, Present Subjunctive, Future, Conditional
Model:	**mener** *to lead* → ①

Verbs like:	**céder, régler, espérer** *etc*
Change:	**é** changes to **è** before **-e, -es, -ent**
Tenses affected:	Present, Present Subjunctive
Model:	**céder** *to yield* → ②

	1 PRESENT (+ SUBJUNCTIVE)	FUTURE
je	**mène**	je **mènerai**
tu	**mènes**	tu **mèneras**
il/elle	**mène**	il **mènera** *etc*
nous	menons	
	(menions)	CONDITIONAL
vous	menez	je **mènerais**
	(meniez)	tu **mènerais**
ils/elles	**mènent**	il **mènerait** *etc*

	2 PRESENT (+ SUBJUNCTIVE)
je	**cède**
tu	**cèdes**
il/elle	**cède**
nous	cédons
	(cédions)
vous	cédez
	(cédiez)
ils/elles	**cèdent**

□ The Imperative

The imperative is the form of the verb used to give commands or orders. It can be used politely, as in English 'Shut the door, please'.

The imperative is the same as the present tense **tu, nous** and **vous** forms without the subject pronouns:

donne*	**finis**	**vends**
give	*finish*	*sell*

*The final 's' of the present tense of first conjugation verbs is dropped, except before **y** and **en** → ①

donnons	**finissons**	**vendons**
let's give	*let's finish*	*let's sell*

donnez	**finissez**	**vendez**
give	*finish*	*sell*

- The imperative of irregular verbs is given in the verb tables, pp 74 ff.

- Position of object pronouns with the imperative:
  in POSITIVE commands: they follow the verb and are attached to it by hyphens → ②
  in NEGATIVE commands: they precede the verb and are not attached to it → ③

- For the order of object pronouns, see p 170.

- For reflexive verbs – e.g. **se lever** *to get up* – the object pronoun is the reflexive pronoun → ④

1. Compare: **Tu donnes de l'argent à Paul**
   You give (some) money to Paul

   and: **Donne de l'argent à Paul**
   Give (some) money to Paul

2. **Excusez-moi**
   Excuse me
   Crois-nous
   Believe us
   Attendons-la
   Let's wait for her/it

   Envoyons-les-leur
   Let's send them to them
   Expliquez-le-moi
   Explain it to me
   Rends-la-lui
   Give it back to him/her

3. **Ne me dérange pas**
   Don't disturb me
   Ne les négligeons pas
   Let's not neglect them
   Ne leur répondez pas
   Don't answer them

   Ne leur en parlons pas
   Let's not speak to them about it
   N'y pense plus
   Don't think about it any more
   Ne la lui rends pas
   Don't give it back to him/her

4. **Lève-toi**
   Get up
   Dépêchons-nous
   Let's hurry
   Levez-vous
   Get up

   Ne te lève pas
   Don't get up
   Ne nous affolons pas
   Let's not panic
   Ne vous levez pas
   Don't get up

▢ Compound Tenses: formation

In French the compound tenses are:

Perfect	→ ①
Pluperfect	→ ②
Future Perfect	→ ③
Conditional Perfect	→ ④
Past Anterior	→ ⑤
Perfect Subjunctive	→ ⑥
Pluperfect Subjunctive	→ ⑦

They consist of the past participle of the verb together with an auxiliary verb. Most verbs take the auxiliary **avoir**, but some take **être** (see p 28).

Compound tenses are formed in exactly the same way for both regular and irregular verbs, the only difference being that irregular verbs may have an irregular past participle.

▢ The Past Participle

For all compound tenses you need to know how to form the past participle of the verb. For regular verbs this is as follows:

- 1st conjugation: replace the **-er** of the infinitive by **-é** → ⑧

- 2nd conjugation: replace the **-ir** of the infinitive by **-i** → ⑨

- 3rd conjugation: replace the **-re** of the infinitive by **-u** → ⑩

- See p 50 for agreement of past participles.

with **avoir**	with **être**

1   **j'ai donné**
I gave, have given

je suis tombé
I fell, have fallen

2   **j'avais donné**
I had given

j'étais tombé
I had fallen

3   **j'aurai donné**
I shall have given

je serai tombé
I shall have fallen

4   **j'aurais donné**
I should /would have given

je serais tombé
I should/would have fallen

5   **j'eus donné**
I had given

je fus tombé
I had fallen

6   **(que) j'aie donné**
(that) I gave, have given

(que) je sois tombé
(that) I fell, have fallen

7   **(que) j'eusse donné**
(that) I had given

(que) je fusse tombé
(that) I had fallen

8   **donner** → **donné**
to give   given

9   **finir** → **fini**
to finish   finished

10   **vendre** → **vendu**
to sell   sold

❐ Compound Tenses: formation *(Continued)*

Verbs taking the auxiliary avoir

Perfect tense: the present tense of **avoir** plus the past participle → 1

Pluperfect tense: the imperfect tense of **avoir** plus the past participle → 2

Future Perfect: the future tense of **avoir** plus the past participle → 3

Conditional Perfect: the conditional of **avoir** plus the past participle → 4

Past Anterior: the past historic of **avoir** plus the past participle → 5

Perfect Subjunctive: the present subjunctive of **avoir** plus the past participle → 6

Pluperfect Subjunctive: the imperfect subjunctive of **avoir** plus the past participle → 7

- For how to form the past participle of regular verbs see p 22. The past participle of irregular verbs is given for each verb in the verb tables, pp 74 ff.

- The past participle must agree in number and in gender with any preceding direct object (see p 50).

1 PERFECT

j'ai donné	nous avons donné
tu as donné	vous avez donné
il/elle a donné	ils/elles ont donné

2 PLUPERFECT

j'avais donné	nous avions donné
tu avais donné	vous aviez donné
il/elle avait donné	ils/elles avaient donné

3 FUTURE PERFECT

j'aurai donné	nous aurons donné
tu auras donné	vous aurez donné
il/elle aura donné	ils/elles auront donné

4 CONDITIONAL PERFECT

j'aurais donné	nous aurions donné
tu aurais donné	vous auriez donné
il/elle aurait donné	ils/elles auraient donné

5 PAST ANTERIOR

j'eus donné	nous eûmes donné
tu eus donné	vous eûtes donné
il/elle eut donné	ils/elles eurent donné

6 PERFECT SUBJUNCTIVE

j'aie donné	nous ayons donné
tu aies donné	vous ayez donné
il/elle ait donné	ils/elles aient donné

7 PLUPERFECT SUBJUNCTIVE

j'eusse donné	nous eussions donné
tu eusses donné	vous eussiez donné
il/elle eût donné	ils/elles eussent donné

◻ Compound Tenses: formation *(Continued)*

Verbs taking the auxiliary être

Perfect tense:	the present tense of **être** plus the past participle → 1
Pluperfect tense:	the imperfect tense of **être** plus the past participle → 2
Future Perfect:	the future tense of **être** plus the past participle → 3
Conditional Perfect:	the conditional of **être** plus the past participle → 4
Past Anterior:	the past historic of **être** plus the past participle → 5
Perfect Subjunctive:	the present subjunctive of **être** plus the past participle → 6
Pluperfect Subjunctive:	the imperfect subjunctive of **être** plus the past participle → 7

+ For how to form the past participle of regular verbs see p 22. The past participle of irregular verbs is given for each verb in the verb tables, pp 74 ff.

◆ For agreement of past participles, see p 50.

◆ For a list of verbs and verb types that take the auxiliary **être**, see p 28.

Examples

1. **PERFECT**

je suis tombé(e)	nous sommes tombé(e)s
tu es tombé(e)	vous êtes tombé(e)(s)
il est tombé	ils sont tombés
elle est tombée	elles sont tombées

2. **PLUPERFECT**

j'étais tombé(e)	nous étions tombé(e)s
tu étais tombé(e)	vous étiez tombé(e)(s)
il était tombé	ils étaient tombés
elle était tombée	elles étaient tombées

3. **FUTURE PERFECT**

je serai tombé(e)	nous serons tombé(e)s
tu seras tombé(e)	vous serez tombé(e)(s)
il sera tombé	ils seront tombés
elle sera tombée	elles seront tombées

4. **CONDITIONAL PERFECT**

je serais tombé(e)	nous serions tombé(e)s
tu serais tombé(e)	vous seriez tombé(e)(s)
il serait tombé	ils seraient tombés
elle serait tombée	elles seraient tombées

5. **PAST ANTERIOR**

je fus tombé(e)	nous fûmes tombé(e)s
tu fus tombé(e)	vous fûtes tombé(e)(s)
il fut tombé	ils furent tombés
elle fut tombée	elles furent tombées

6. **PERFECT SUBJUNCTIVE**

je sois tombé(e)	nous soyons tombé(e)s
tu sois tombé(e)	vous soyez tombé(e)(s)
il soit tombé	ils soient tombés
elle soit tombée	elles soient tombées

7. **PLUPERFECT SUBJUNCTIVE**

je fusse tombé(e)	nous fussions tombé(e)s
tu fusses tombé(e)	vous fussiez tombé(e)(s)
il fût tombé	ils fussent tombés
elle fût tombée	elles fussent tombées

❏ Compound Tenses *(Continued)*

The following verbs take the auxiliary être

- Reflexive verbs (see p 30) → 1

- The following intransitive verbs (i.e. verbs which cannot take a direct object), largely expressing motion or a change of state:

aller	*to go* → 2	**passer**	*to pass*
arriver	*to arrive; to happen*	**rentrer**	*to go back/in*
descendre	*to go/come down*	**rester**	*to stay* → 5
devenir	*to become*	**retourner**	*to go back*
entrer	*to go/come in*	**revenir**	*to come back*
monter	*to go/come up*	**sortir**	*to go/come out*
mourir	*to die* → 3	**tomber**	*to fall*
naître	*to be born*	**venir**	*to come* → 6
partir	*to leave* → 4		

- Of these, the following are conjugated with **avoir** when used transitively (i.e. with a direct object):

descendre	*to bring/take down*
entrer	*to bring/take in*
monter	*to bring/take up* → 7
passer	*to pass; to spend* → 8
rentrer	*to bring/take in*
retourner	*to turn over*
sortir	*to bring/take out* → 9

⚠ NOTE that the past participle must show an agreement in number and gender whenever the auxiliary is **être** EXCEPT FOR REFLEXIVE VERBS WHERE THE REFLEXIVE PRONOUN IS THE INDIRECT OBJECT (see p 50).

Grammar

1 **je me suis arrêté(e)**
I stopped
tu t'es levé(e)
you got up

    elle s'est trompée
she made a mistake
ils s'étaient battus
they had fought (one another)

2 **elle est allée**
she went

3 **ils sont morts**
they died

4 **vous êtes partie**
you left *(addressing a female person)*
vous êtes parties
you left *(addressing more than one female person)*

5 **nous sommes resté(e)s**
we stayed

6 **elles étaient venues**
they [female] had come

7 **Il a monté les valises**
He's taken up the cases

8 **Nous avons passé trois semaines chez elle**
We spent three weeks at her place

9 **Avez-vous sorti la voiture?**
Have you taken the car out?

❑ Reflexive Verbs

A reflexive verb is one accompanied by a reflexive pronoun, e.g. **se lever** *to get up*; **se laver** *to wash (oneself)*. The pronouns are:

PERSON	SINGULAR	PLURAL
1st	**me (m')**	**nous**
2nd	**te (t')**	**vous**
3rd	**se (s')**	**se (s')**

The forms shown in brackets are used before a vowel, an **h** 'mute', or the pronoun **y** → 1

- In positive commands, **te** changes to **toi** → 2

- The reflexive pronoun 'reflects back' to the subject, but it is not always translated in English → 3

  The plural pronouns are sometimes translated as *one another, each other* (the 'reciprocal' meaning) → 4

  The reciprocal meaning may be emphasized by **l'un(e) l'autre (les un(e)s les autres)** → 5

- Simple tenses of reflexive verbs are conjugated in exactly the same way as those of non-reflexive verbs except that the reflexive pronoun is always used. Compound tenses are formed with the auxiliary **être**. A sample reflexive verb is conjugated in full on pp 34 and 35.

  For agreement of past participles, see p 32.

Position of Reflexive Pronouns

- In constructions other than the imperative affirmative the pronoun comes before the verb → 6

- In the imperative affirmative, the pronoun follows the verb and is attached to it by a hyphen → 7

1. **Je m'ennuie**
   I'm bored
   Elle s'habille
   She's getting dressed
   Ils s'y intéressent
   They are interested in it

2. **Assieds-toi**
   Sit down
   Tais-toi
   Be quiet

3. **Je me prépare**
   I'm getting (myself) ready
   Nous nous lavons
   We're washing (ourselves)
   Elle se lève
   She gets up

4. **Nous nous parlons**
   We speak to each other
   Ils se ressemblent
   They resemble one another

5. **Ils se regardent l'un l'autre**
   They are looking at each other

6. **Je me couche tôt**
   I go to bed early
   Comment vous appelez-vous?
   What is your name?
   Il ne s'est pas rasé
   He hasn't shaved
   Ne te dérange pas pour nous
   Don't put yourself out on our account

7. **Dépêche-toi**
   Hurry (up)
   Renseignons-nous
   Let's find out
   Asseyez-vous
   Sit down

Grammar

❏ **Reflexive Verbs** *(Continued)*

Past Participle Agreement

- In most reflexive verbs the reflexive pronoun is a DIRECT object pronoun → ⒈

- When a direct object accompanies the reflexive verb the pronoun is then the INDIRECT object → ⒉

- The past participle of a reflexive verb agrees in number and gender with a direct object which *precedes* the verb (usually, but not always, the reflexive pronoun) → ⒊

  The past participle does not change if the direct object follows the verb → ⒋

Here are some common reflexive verbs:

s'en aller	*to go away*	**se hâter**	*to hurry*
s'amuser	*to enjoy oneself*	**se laver**	*to wash (oneself)*
s'appeler	*to be called*	**se lever**	*to get up*
s'arrêter	*to stop*	**se passer**	*to happen*
s'asseoir	*to sit (down)*	**se promener**	*to go for a walk*
se baigner	*to go swimming*	**se rappeler**	*to remember*
se blesser	*to hurt oneself*	**se ressembler**	*to resemble each other*
se coucher	*to go to bed*	**se retourner**	*to turn round*
se demander	*to wonder*	**se réveiller**	*to wake up*
se dépêcher	*to hurry*	**se sauver**	*to run away*
se diriger	*to make one's way*	**se souvenir de**	*to remember*
s'endormir	*to fall asleep*	**se taire**	*to be quiet*
s'ennuyer	*to be/get bored*	**se tromper**	*to be mistaken*
se fâcher	*to get angry*	**se trouver**	*to be (situated)*
s'habiller	*to dress (oneself)*		

☐ **Je m'appelle**
I'm called *(literally: I call myself)*
Asseyez-vous
Sit down *(literally: Seat yourself)*
Ils se lavent
They wash (themselves)

② **Elle se lave les mains**
She's washing her hands *(literally: She's washing to herself the hands)*
Je me brosse les dents
I brush my teeth
Nous nous envoyons des cadeaux à Noël
We send presents to each other at Christmas

③ **'Je me suis endormi' s'est-il excusé**
'I fell asleep', he apologized
Pauline s'est dirigée vers la sortie
Pauline made her way towards the exit
Ils se sont levés vers dix heures
They got up around ten o'clock
Elles se sont excusées de leur erreur
They apologized for their mistake
Est-ce que tu t'es blessée, Cécile?
Have you hurt yourself, Cécile?

④ **Elle s'est lavé les cheveux**
She (has) washed her hair
Nous nous sommes serré la main
We shook hands
Christine s'est cassé la jambe
Christine has broken her leg

□ **Reflexive Verbs** *(Continued)*

Conjugation of: **se laver** *to wash (oneself)*

I SIMPLE TENSES	
PRESENT	
je me lave	nous nous lavons
tu te laves	vous vous lavez
il/elle se lave	ils/elles se lavent
IMPERFECT	
je me lavais	nous nous lavions
tu te lavais	vous vous laviez
il/elle se lavait	ils/elles se lavaient
FUTURE	
je me laverai	nous nous laverons
tu te laveras	vous vous laverez
il/elle se lavera	ils/elles se laveront
CONDITIONAL	
je me laverais	nous nous laverions
tu te laverais	vous vous laveriez
il/elle se laverait	ils/elles se laveraient
PAST HISTORIC	
je me lavai	nous nous lavâmes
tu te lavas	vous vous lavâtes
il/elle se lava	ils/elles se lavèrent
PRESENT SUBJUNCTIVE	
je me lave	nous nous lavions
tu te laves	vous vous laviez
il/elle se lave	ils/elles se lavent
IMPERFECT SUBJUNCTIVE	
je me lavasse	nous nous lavassions
tu te lavasses	vous vous lavassiez
il/elle se lavât	ils/elles se lavassent

□ **Reflexive Verbs** *(Continued)*

Conjugation of: **se laver** *to wash (oneself)*

II COMPOUND TENSES

PERFECT

je me suis lavé(e)	nous nous sommes lavé(e)s
tu t'es lavé(e)	vous vous êtes lavé(e)(s)
il/elle s'est lavé(e)	ils/elles se sont lavé(e)s

PLUPERFECT

je m'étais lavé(e)	nous nous étions lavé(e)s
tu t'étais lavé(e)	vous vous étiez lavé(e)(s)
il/elle s'était lavé(e)	ils/elles s'étaient lavé(e)s

FUTURE PERFECT

je me serai lavé(e)	nous nous serons lavé(e)s
tu te seras lavé(e)	vous vous serez lavé(e)(s)
il/elle se sera lavé(e)	ils/elles se seront lavé(e)s

CONDITIONAL PERFECT

je me serais lavé(e)	nous nous serions lavé(e)s
tu te serais lavé(e)	vous vous seriez lavé(e)(s)
il/elle se serait lavé(e)	ils/elles se seraient lavé(e)s

PAST ANTERIOR

je me fus lavé(e)	nous nous fûmes lavé(e)s
tu te fus lavé(e)	vous vous fûtes lavé(e)(s)
il/elle se fut lavé(e)	ils/elles se furent lavé(e)s

PERFECT SUBJUNCTIVE

je me sois lavé(e)	nous nous soyons lavé(e)s
tu te sois lavé(e)	vous vous soyez lavé(e)(s)
il/elle se soit lavé(e)	ils/elles se soient lavé(e)s

PLUPERFECT SUBJUNCTIVE

je me fusse lavé(e)	nous nous fussions lavé(e)s
tu te fusses lavé(e)	vous vous fussiez lavé(e)(s)
il/elle se fût lavé(e)	ils/elles se fussent lavé(e)s

◻ The Passive

In the passive, the subject *receives* the action (e.g. *I was hit*) as opposed to *performing* it (e.g. *I hit him*). In English the verb 'to be' is used with the past participle. In French the passive is formed in exactly the same way, i.e.:

a tense of **être** + past participle.

The past participle agrees in number and gender with the subject → 1

A sample verb is conjugated in the passive voice on pp 38 and 39.

◆ The indirect object in French cannot become the subject in the passive:

in **quelqu'un m'a donné un livre** the indirect object **m'** cannot become the subject of a passive verb (unlike English: *someone gave me a book* → *I was given a book*).

◆ The passive meaning is often expressed in French by:

– **on** plus a verb in the active voice → 2
– a reflexive verb (see p 30) → 3

1. **Philippe a été récompensé**
Phillip has been rewarded
Cette peinture est très admirée
This painting is greatly admired
Ils le feront pourvu qu'ils soient payés
They'll do it provided they're paid
Les enfants seront félicités
The children will be congratulated
Cette mesure aurait été critiquée si ...
This measure would have been criticized if ...
Les portes avaient été fermées
The doors had been closed

2. **On leur a envoyé une lettre**
They were sent a letter
On nous a montré le jardin
We were shown the garden
On m'a dit que ...
I was told that ...

3. **Ils se vendent 30 francs (la) pièce**
They are sold for 30 francs each
Ce mot ne s'emploie plus
This word is no longer used

❏ The Passive *(Continued)*

Conjugation of: **être aimé** to *be liked*

PRESENT	
je suis aimé(e)	nous sommes aimé(e)s
tu es aimé(e)	vous êtes aimé(e)(s)
il/elle est aimé(e)	ils/elles sont aimé(e)s
IMPERFECT	
j'étais aimé(e)	nous étions aimé(e)s
tu étais aimé(e)	vous étiez aimé(e)(s)
il/elle était aimé(e)	ils/elles étaient aimé(e)s
FUTURE	
je serai aimé(e)	nous serons aimé(e)s
tu seras aimé(e)	vous serez aimé(e)(s)
il/elle sera aimé(e)	ils/elles seront aimé(e)s
CONDITIONAL	
je serais aimé(e)	nous serions aimé(e)s
tu serais aimé(e)	vous seriez aimé(e)(s)
il/elle serait aimé(e)	ils/elles seraient aimé(e)s
PAST HISTORIC	
je fus aimé(e)	nous fûmes aimé(e)s
tu fus aimé(e)	vous fûtes aimé(e)(s)
il/elle fut aimé(e)	ils/elles furent aimé(e)s
PRESENT SUBJUNCTIVE	
je sois aimé(e)	nous soyons aimé(e)s
tu sois aimé(e)	vous soyez aimé(e)(s)
il/elle soit aimé(e)	ils/elles soient aimé(e)s
IMPERFECT SUBJUNCTIVE	
je fusse aimé(e)	nous fussions aimé(e)s
tu fusses aimé(e)	vous fussiez aimé(e)(s)
il/elle fût aimé(e)	ils/elles fussent aimé(e)s

◻ The Passive *(Continued)*

Conjugation of: **être aimé** to *be liked*

PERFECT
j'ai été aimé(e)   nous avons été aimé(e)s
tu as été aimé(e)   vous avez été aimé(e)(s)
il/elle a été aimé(e)   ils/elles ont été aimé(e)s

PLUPERFECT
j'avais été aimé(e)   nous avions été aimé(e)s
tu avais été aimé(e)   vous aviez été aimé(e)(s)
il/elle avait été aimé(e)   ils/elles avaient été aimé(e)s

FUTURE PERFECT
j'aurai été aimé(e)   nous aurons été aimé(e)s
tu auras été aimé(e)   vous aurez été aimé(e)(s)
il/elle aura été aimé(e)   ils/elles auront été aimé(e)s

CONDITIONAL PERFECT
j'aurais été aimé(e)   nous aurions été aimé(e)s
tu aurais été aimé(e)   vous auriez été aimé(e)(s)
il/elle aurait été aimé(e)   ils/elles auraient été aimé(e)s

PAST ANTERIOR
j'eus été aimé(e)   nous eûmes été aimé(e)s
tu eus été aimé(e)   vous eûtes été aimé(e)(s)
il/elle eut été aimé(e)   ils/elles eurent été aimé(e)s

PERFECT SUBJUNCTIVE
j'aie été aimé(e)   nous ayons été aimé(e)s
tu aies été aimé(e)   vous ayez été aimé(e)(s)
il/elle ait été aimé(e)   ils/elles aient été aimé(e)s

PLUPERFECT SUBJUNCTIVE
j'eusse été aimé(e)   nous eussions été aimé(e)s
tu eusses été aimé(e)   vous eussiez été aimé(e)(s)
il/elle eût été aimé(e)   ils/elles eussent été aimé(e)s

□ Impersonal Verbs

Impersonal verbs are used only in the infinitive and in the third person singular with the subject pronoun **il**, generally translated *it*.

e.g. **il pleut**
it's raining
il est facile de dire que …
it's easy to say that …

The most common impersonal verbs are:

INFINITIVE	CONSTRUCTIONS
s'agir	**il s'agit de** + noun → $\boxed{1}$ *it's a question/matter of something,* *it's about something* **il s'agit de** + infinitive → $\boxed{2}$ *it's a question/matter of doing; somebody must do*
falloir	**il faut** + noun object (+ indirect object) → $\boxed{3}$ *(somebody) needs something, something is* *necessary (to somebody)* **il faut** + infinitive (+ indirect object) → $\boxed{4}$ *it is necessary to do* **il faut que** + subjunctive → $\boxed{5}$ *it is necessary to do, somebody must do*
grêler	**il grêle** *it's hailing*
neiger	**il neige** *it's snowing* → $\boxed{6}$
pleuvoir	**il pleut** *it's raining*
tonner	**il tonne** *it's thundering*
valoir mieux	**il vaut mieux** + infinitive → $\boxed{7}$ *it's better to do* **il vaut mieux que** + subjunctive → $\boxed{8}$ *it's better to do/that somebody does*

① **Il ne s'agit pas d'argent**
It isn't a question/matter of money
De quoi s'agit-il?
What is it about?
Il s'agit de la vie d'une famille au début du siècle
It's about the life of a family at the turn of the century

② **Il s'agit de faire vite**
We must act quickly

③ **Il faut du courage pour faire ça**
One needs courage to do that; Courage is needed to do that
Il me faut une chaise de plus
I need an extra chair

④ **Il faut partir**
It is necessary to leave; We/I/You must leave*
Il me fallait prendre une décision
I had to make a decision

⑤ **Il faut que vous partiez**
You have to leave/You must leave
Il faudrait que je fasse mes valises
I should have to/ought to pack my cases

⑥ **Il pleuvait à verse**
It was raining heavily/It was pouring

⑦ **Il vaut mieux refuser**
It's better to refuse; You/He/I had better refuse*
Il vaudrait mieux rester
You/We/She had better stay*

⑧ **Il vaudrait mieux que nous ne venions pas**
It would be better if we didn't come; We'd better not come

The translation here obviously depends on context

◻ Impersonal Verbs *(Continued)*

The following verbs are also commonly used in impersonal constructions:

INFINITIVE	CONSTRUCTIONS
avoir	**il y a** + noun → 1 *there is/are*
être	**il est** + noun → 2 *it is, there are* (very literary style) **il est** + adjective + **de** + infinitive → 3 *it is*
faire	**il fait** + adjective of weather → 4 *it is* **il fait** + noun depicting weather/dark/light *etc* *it is* → 5
manquer	**il manque** + noun (+ indirect object) → 6 *there is/are … missing, something is missing/lacking*
paraître	**il paraît que** + subjunctive → 7 *it seems/appears that* **il paraît** + indirect object + **que** + indicative → 8 *it seems/appears to somebody that*
rester	**il reste** + noun (+ indirect object) → 9 *there is/are … left, (somebody) has something left*
sembler	**il semble que** + subjunctive → 10 *it seems/appears that* **il semble** + indirect object + **que** + indicative → 11 *it seems/appears to somebody that*
suffire	**il suffit de** + infinitive → 12 *it is enough to do* **il suffit de** + noun → 13 *something is enough, it only takes something*

1. **Il y a du pain (qui reste)**
   There is some bread (left)
   Il n'y avait pas de lettres ce matin
   There were no letters this morning

2. **Il est dix heures**
   It's ten o'clock
   Il est des gens qui ...
   There are (some) people who ...

3. **Il était inutile de protester**
   It was useless to protest
   Il est facile de critiquer
   Criticizing is easy

4. **Il fait beau/mauvais**
   It's lovely/horrible weather

5. **Il faisait du soleil/du vent**
   It was sunny/windy
   Il fait jour/nuit
   It's light/dark

6. **Il manque deux tasses**
   There are two cups missing; Two cups are missing
   Il manquait un bouton à sa chemise
   His shirt had a button missing

7. **Il paraît qu'ils partent demain**
   It appears they are leaving tomorrow

8. **Il nous paraît certain qu'il aura du succès**
   It seems certain to us that he'll be successful

9. **Il reste deux miches de pain**
   There are two loaves left
   Il lui restait cinquante francs
   He/She had fifty francs left

10. **Il semble que vous ayez raison**
    It seems that you are right

11. **Il me semblait qu'il conduisait trop vite**
    It seemed to me (that) he was driving too fast

12. **Il suffit de téléphoner pour réserver une place**
    You need only phone to reserve a seat

13. **Il suffit d'une seule erreur pour tout gâcher**
    One single error is enough to ruin everything

◻ The Infinitive

The infinitive is the form of the verb found in dictionary entries meaning 'to ... ', e.g. **donner** *to give,* **vivre** *to live.*

There are three main types of verbal construction involving the infinitive:

- with no linking preposition → 1
- with the linking preposition **à** → 2 (see also p 64)
- with the linking preposition **de** → 3 (see also p 64)

Verbs followed by an infinitive with no linking preposition

- **devoir, pouvoir, savoir, vouloir** and **falloir** (i.e. modal auxiliary verbs: p 52 → 1).
- **valoir mieux**: see Impersonal Verbs, p 40.
- verbs of seeing or hearing e.g. **voir** *to see,* **entendre** *to hear* → 4
- intransitive verbs of motion e.g. **aller** *to go,* **descendre** *to come/go down* → 5
- **envoyer** *to send* → 6
- **faillir** → 7
- **faire** → 8
- **laisser** *to let, allow* → 9
- The following common verbs:

adorer	*to love*
aimer	*to like, love* → 10
aimer mieux	*to prefer* → 11
compter	*to expect*
désirer	*to wish, want* → 12
détester	*to hate* → 13
espérer	*to hope* → 14
oser	*to dare* → 15
préférer	*to prefer*
sembler	*to seem* → 16
souhaiter	*to wish*

Grammar

☐1 **Voulez-vous attendre?**
Would you like to wait?

☐2 **J'apprends à nager**
I'm learning to swim

☐3 **Essayez de venir**
Try to come

☐4 **Il nous a vus arriver**
He saw us arriving
On les entend chanter
You can hear them singing

☐5 **Allez voir Nicolas**
Go and see Nicholas
Descends leur demander
Go down and ask them

☐6 **Je l'ai envoyé les voir**
I sent him to see them

☐7 **J'ai failli tomber**
I almost fell

☐8 **Ne me faites pas rire!**
Don't make me laugh!
J'ai fait réparer ma valise
I've had my case repaired

☐9 **Laissez-moi passer**
Let me pass

☐10 **Il aime nous accompagner**
He likes to come with us

☐11 **J'aimerais mieux le choisir moi-même**
I'd rather choose it myself

☐12 **Elle ne désire pas venir**
She doesn't wish to come

☐13 **Je déteste me lever le matin**
I hate getting up in the morning

☐14 **Espérez-vous aller en vacances?**
Are you hoping to go on holiday?

☐15 **Nous n'avons pas osé y retourner**
We haven't dared go back

☐16 **Vous semblez être inquiet**
You seem to be worried

☐ The Infinitive: Set Expressions

The following are set in French with the meaning shown:

aller chercher	*to go for, to go and get*	→ 1
envoyer chercher	*to send for*	→ 2
entendre dire que	*to hear it said that*	→ 3
entendre parler de	*to hear of/about*	→ 4
faire entrer	*to show in*	→ 5
faire sortir	*to let out*	→ 6
faire venir	*to send for*	→ 7
laisser tomber	*to drop*	→ 8
vouloir dire	*to mean*	→ 9

The Perfect Infinitive

- The perfect infinitive is formed using the auxiliary verb **avoir** or **être** as appropriate with the past participle of the verb → 10

- The perfect infinitive is found:

  – following the preposition **après** *after* → 11
  – following certain verbal constructions → 12

1. **Va chercher tes photos**
   Go and get your photos
   Il est allé chercher Alexandre
   He's gone to get Alexander

2. **J'ai envoyé chercher un médecin**
   I've sent for a doctor

3. **J'ai entendu dire qu'il est malade**
   I've heard it said that he's ill

4. **Je n'ai plus entendu parler de lui**
   I didn't hear anything more (said) of him

5. **Fais entrer nos invités**
   Show our guests in

6. **J'ai fait sortir le chat**
   I've let the cat out

7. **Je vous ai fait venir parce que ...**
   I sent for you because ...

8. **Il a laissé tomber le vase**
   He dropped the vase

9. **Qu'est-ce que cela veut dire?**
   What does that mean?

10. **avoir fini**   **être allé**   **s'être levé**
    to have finished   to have gone   to have got up

11. **Après avoir pris cette décision, il nous a appelé**
    After making/having made that decision, he called us
    Après être sorties, elles se sont dirigées vers le parking
    After leaving/having left, they headed for the car park
    Après nous être levé(e)s, nous avons lu les journaux
    After getting up/having got up, we read the papers

12. **pardonner à qn d'avoir fait**
    to forgive sb for doing/having done
    remercier qn d'avoir fait
    to thank sb for doing/having done
    regretter d'avoir fait
    to be sorry for doing/having done

□ The Present Participle

Formation

+ 1st conjugation
  Replace the **-er** of the infinitive by **-ant** → ☐1
  – Verbs ending in **-cer**: **c** changes to **ç** → ☐2
  – Verbs ending in **-ger**: **g** changes to **ge** → ☐3
+ 2nd conjugation
  Replace the **-ir** of the infinitive by **-issant** → ☐4
+ 3rd conjugation
  Replace the **-re** of the infinitive by **-ant** → ☐5
+ For irregular present participles, see irregular verbs, pp 74 ff.

Uses

The present participle has a more restricted use in French than in English.

+ Used as a verbal form, the present participle is invariable. It is found:
  – on its own, where it corresponds to the English present participle → ☐6
  – following the preposition **en** → ☐7

  ⚠ NOTE, in particular, the construction:

  verb + **en** + present participle

  which is often translated by an English phrasal verb, i.e. one followed by a preposition like *to run down, to bring up* → ☐8

+ Used as an adjective, the present participle agrees in number and gender with the noun or pronoun → ☐9

  ⚠ NOTE, in particular, the use of **ayant** and **étant** – the present participles of the auxiliary verbs **avoir** and **être** – with a past participle → ☐10

1	**donner**	→	**donnant**
	to give		giving
2	**lancer**	→	**lançant**
	to throw		throwing
3	**manger**	→	**mangeant**
	to eat		eating
4	**finir**	→	**finissant**
	to finish		finishing
5	**vendre**	→	**vendant**
	to sell		selling

6   **David, habitant près de Paris, a la possibilité de ...**
David, living near Paris, has the opportunity of…

Elle, pensant que je serais fâché, a dit '...'
She, thinking that I would be angry, said '…'

Ils m'ont suivi, criant à tue-tête
They followed me, shouting at the top of their voices

7   **En attendant sa sœur, Richard s'est endormi**
While waiting for his sister, Richard fell asleep

Téléphone-nous an arrivant chez toi
Telephone us when you get home

En appuyant sur ce bouton, on peut ...
By pressing this button, you can …

Il s'est blessé en essayant de sauver un chat
He hurt himself trying to rescue a cat

8   **sortir en courant**
to run out *(literally: to go out running)*

avancer en boîtant
to limp along *(literally: to go forward limping)*

9   **le soleil couchant**   **une lumière éblouissante**
the setting sun   a dazzling light

ils sont déroutants   **elles étaient étonnantes**
they are disconcerting   they were surprising

10   **Ayant mangé plus tôt, il a pu ...**
Having eaten earlier, he was able to …

Étant arrivée en retard, elle a dû ...
Having arrived late, she had to …

◻ Past Participle Agreement

Like adjectives, a past participle must sometimes agree in number and gender with a noun or pronoun. For the rules of agreement, see below.
Example: **donné**

	MASCULINE	FEMININE
SING.	donné	donné**e**
PLUR.	donné**s**	donné**es**

- When the masculine singular form already ends in **-s**, no further **s** is added in the masculine plural, e.g. **pris** *taken*.

Rules of Agreement in Compound Tenses

- When the auxiliary verb is **avoir**

  The past participle remains in the masculine singular form, unless a direct object precedes the verb. The past participle then agrees in number and gender with the preceding direct object → ①

- When the auxiliary verb is **être**

  The past participle of a non-reflexive verb agrees in number and gender with the subject → ②

  The past participle of a reflexive verb agrees in number and gender with the reflexive pronoun, if the pronoun is a direct object → ③

  No agreement is made if the reflexive pronoun is an indirect object → ④

The Past Participle as an adjective

The past participle agrees in number and gender with the noun or pronoun → ⑤

1. **Voici le livre que vous avez demandé**
Here's the book you asked for
Laquelle avaient-elles choisie?
Which one had they chosen?
Ces amis? Je les ai rencontrés à Édimbourg
Those friends? I met them in Edinburgh
Il a gardé toutes les lettres qu'elle a écrites
He has kept all the letters she wrote

2. **Est-ce que ton frère est allé à l'étranger?**
Did your brother go abroad?
Elle était restée chez elle
She had stayed at home
Ils sont partis dans la matinée
They left in the morning
Mes cousines sont revenues hier
My cousins came back yesterday

3. **Tu t'es rappelé d'acheter du pain, Georges?**
Did you remember to buy bread, George?
Martine s'est demandée pourquoi il l'appelait
Martine wondered why he was calling her
'Lui et moi nous nous sommes cachés' a-t-elle dit
'He and I hid,' she said
Les vendeuses se sont mises en grève
Shop assistants have gone on strike
Vous vous êtes brouillés?
Have you fallen out with each other?
Les ouvrières s'étaient entraidées
The workers had helped one another

4. **Elle s'est lavé les mains**
She washed her hands
Ils se sont parlé pendant des heures
They talked to each other for hours

5. **à un moment donné**   **la porte ouverte**
at a given time   the open door
ils sont bien connus   **elles semblent fatiguées**
they are well-known   they seem tired

◻ Modal Auxiliary Verbs

● In French, the modal auxiliary verbs are: **devoir**, **pouvoir**, **savoir**, **vouloir** and **falloir**.

● They are followed by a verb in the infinitive and have the following meanings:

devoir
    to have to, must → 1
    to be due to → 2
    in the conditional/conditional perfect:
    should/should have, ought/ought to have → 3

pouvoir
    to be able to, can → 4
    to be allowed to, can, may → 5
    indicating possibility: *may/might/could* → 6

savoir
    to know how to, can → 7

vouloir
    to want/wish to → 8
    to be willing to, will → 9
    in polite phrases → 10

falloir
    to be necessary: see Impersonal Verbs, p 40.

1. **Je dois leur rendre visite**
   I must visit them
   Elle a dû partir
   She (has) had to leave
   Il a dû regretter d'avoir parlé
   He must have been sorry he spoke

2. **Vous devez revenir demain**
   You're due (to come) back tomorrow
   Je devais attraper le train de neuf heures mais ...
   I was (supposed) to catch the nine o'clock train but ...

3. **Je devrais le faire**
   I ought to do it
   J'aurais dû m'excuser
   I ought to have apologized

4. **Il ne peut pas lever le bras**
   He can't raise his arm
   Pouvez-vous réparer cette montre?
   Can you mend this watch?

5. **Puis-je les accompagner?**
   May I go with them?

6. **Il peut encore changer d'avis**
   He may change his mind yet
   Cela pourrait être vrai
   It could/might be true

7. **Savez-vous conduire?**
   Can you drive?
   Je ne sais pas faire une omelette
   I don't know how to make an omelette

8. **Elle veut rester encore un jour**
   She wants to stay another day

9. **Ils ne voulaient pas le faire**
   They wouldn't do it/They weren't willing to do it
   Ma voiture ne veut pas démarrer
   My car won't start

10. **Voulez-vous boire quelque chose?**
    Would you like something to drink?

◻ Use of Tenses

The Present

- Unlike English, French does not distinguish between the simple present (e.g. *I smoke, he reads, we live*) and the continuous present (e.g. *I am smoking, he is reading, we are living*) → ①

- To emphasize continuity, the following constructions may be used:

être en train de faire⎱   *to be doing* → ②
être à faire ⎰

- French uses the present tense where English uses the perfect in the following cases:

  – with certain prepositions of time – notably **depuis** *for/since* – when an action begun in the past is continued in the present → ③
Note, however, that the perfect is used as in English when the verb is negative or the action has been completed → ④

  – in the construction **venir de faire** *to have just done* → ⑤

The Future

The future is generally used as in English, but note the following:

- Immediate future time is often expressed by means of the present tense of **aller** plus an infinitive → ⑥

- In time clauses expressing future action, French uses the future where English uses the present → ⑦

The Future Perfect

- Used as in English to mean *shall/will have done* → ⑧

- In time clauses expressing future action, where English uses the perfect tense → ⑨

1 **Je fume**
I smoke OR I am smoking
Il lit
He reads OR He is reading
Nous habitons
We live OR We are living

2 **Il est en train de travailler**
He's (busy) working

3 **Paul apprend à nager depuis six mois**
Paul's been learning to swim for six months *(and still is)*
Je suis debout depuis sept heures
I've been up since seven
Il y a longtemps que vous attendez?
Have you been waiting long?
Voilà deux semaines que nous sommes ici
That's two weeks we've been here *(now)*

4 **Ils ne se sont pas vus depuis des mois**
They haven't seen each other for months
Elle est revenue il y a un an
She came back a year ago

5 **Élisabeth vient de partir**
Elizabeth has just left

6 **Tu vas tomber si tu ne fais pas attention**
You'll fall if you're not careful
Il va manquer le train
He's going to miss the train
Ça va prendre une demi-heure
It'll take half an hour

7 **Quand il viendra vous serez en vacances**
When he comes you'll be on holiday
Faites-nous savoir aussitôt qu'elle arrivera
Let us know as soon as she arrives

8 **J'aurai fini dans une heure**
I shall have finished in an hour

9 **Quand tu auras lu ce roman, rends-le-moi**
When you've read the novel, give it back to me
Je partirai dès que j'aurai fini
I'll leave as soon as I've finished

❏ Use of Tenses (Continued)

The Imperfect

- The imperfect describes:
  - an action (or state) in the past without definite limits in time → ①
  - habitual action(s) in the past (often translated by means of *would* or *used to*) → ②

- French uses the imperfect tense where English uses the pluperfect in the following cases:
  - with certain prepositions of time – notably **depuis** *for/since* – when an action begun in the remoter past was continued in the more recent past → ③
  Note, however, that the pluperfect *is* used as in English, when the verb is negative or the action has been completed → ④
  - in the construction **venir de faire** *to have just done* → ⑤

The Perfect

- The perfect is used to recount a completed action or event in the past. Note that this corresponds to a perfect tense or a simple past tense in English → ⑥

The Past Historic

- Only ever used in *written, literary* French, the past historic recounts a completed action in the past, corresponding to a simple past tense in English → ⑦

The Past Anterior

This tense is used instead of the pluperfect when a verb in another part of the sentence is in the past historic. That is

- in time clauses, after conjunctions like: **quand**, **lorsque** *when*, **dès que**, **aussitôt que** *as soon as*, **après que** *after* → ⑧
- after **à peine** *hardly, scarcely* → ⑨

The Subjunctive

- In spoken French, the present subjunctive generally replaces the imperfect subjunctive. See also pp 58 ff.

1. **Elle regardait par la fenêtre**
   She was looking out of the window
   Il pleuvait quand je suis sorti de chez moi
   It was raining when I left the house
   Nos chambres donnaient sur la plage
   Our rooms overlooked the beach

2. **Dans sa jeunesse, il se levait à l'aube**
   In his youth he got up at dawn
   Nous causions des heures entières
   We would talk for hours on end
   Elle te taquinait, n'est-ce pas?
   She used to tease you, didn't she?

3. **Nous habitions à Londres depuis deux ans**
   We had been living in London for two years *(and still were)*
   Il était malade depuis 1985
   He had been ill since 1985
   Il y avait assez longtemps qu'il le faisait
   He had been doing it for quite a long time

4. **Voilà un an que je ne l'avais pas vu**
   I hadn't seen him for a year
   Il y avait une heure qu'elle était arrivée
   She had arrived one hour before

5. **Je venais de les rencontrer**
   I had just met them

6. **Nous sommes allés au bord de la mer**
   We went/have been to the seaside
   Il a refusé de nous aider
   He (has) refused to help us
   La voiture ne s'est pas arrêtée
   The car didn't stop/hasn't stopped

7. **Le roi mourut en 1592**
   The king died in 1592

8. **Quand il eut fini, il se leva**
   When he had finished, he got up

9. **À peine eut-il parlé qu'on frappa à la porte**
   He had scarcely spoken when there was a knock at the door

❏ The Subjunctive: when to use it

(For how to form the subjunctive see pp 6 ff.)

- After certain conjunctions

quoique ⎱ bien que ⎰	*although* → 1
pour que ⎱ afin que ⎰	*so that* → 2
pourvu que	*provided that* → 3
jusqu'à ce que	*until* → 4
avant que (... ne)	*before* → 5
à moins que (... ne)	*unless* → 6
de peur que (... ne) ⎱ de crainte que (... ne) ⎰	*for fear that, lest* → 7

⚠ NOTE that the **ne** following the conjunctions in examples 5 to 7 has no translation value. It is often omitted in spoken informal French.

- After the conjunctions

de sorte que de façon que de manière que	*so that* (indicating a *purpose*) → 8

When these conjunctions introduce a *result* and not a *purpose*, the subjunctive is not used → 9

- After impersonal constructions which express necessity, possibility etc

il faut que ⎱ il est nécessaire que ⎰	*it is necessary that* → 10
il est possible que	*it is possible that* → 11
il semble que	*it seems that* → 12
il vaut mieux que	*it is better that* → 13
il est dommage que	*it's a pity that* → 14

1   **Bien qu'il fasse beaucoup d'efforts, il est peu récompensé**
Although he makes a lot of effort, he isn't rewarded for it

2   **Demandez un reçu afin que vous puissiez être remboursé**
Ask for a receipt so that you can get a refund

3   **Nous partirons ensemble pourvu que Sylvie soit d'accord**
We'll leave together provided Sylvie agrees

4   **Reste ici jusqu'à ce que nous revenions**
Stay here until we come back

5   **Je le ferai avant que tu ne partes**
I'll do it before you leave

6   **Ce doit être Paul, à moins que je ne me trompe**
That must be Paul, unless I'm mistaken

7   **Parlez bas de peur qu'on ne vous entende**
Speak softly lest anyone hears you

8   **Retournez-vous de sorte que je vous voie**
Turn round so that I can see you

9   **Il refuse de le faire de sorte que je dois le faire moi-même**
He refuses to do it so that I have to do it myself

10   **Il faut que je vous parle immédiatement**
I must speak to you right away/It is necessary that I speak …

11   **Il est possible qu'ils aient raison**
They may be right/It's possible that they are right

12   **Il semble qu'elle ne soit pas venue**
It appears that she hasn't come

13   **Il vaut mieux que vous restiez chez vous**
It's better that you stay at home

14   **Il est dommage qu'elle ait perdu cette adresse**
It's a shame/a pity that she's lost the address

☐ **The Subjunctive: when to use it** *(Continued)*

♦ After verbs of:
  – 'wishing'

vouloir que	
désirer que	*to wish that, want* → 1
souhaiter que	

  – 'fearing'

craindre que	
avoir peur que	*to be afraid that* → 2

  ⚠ NOTE that **ne** in the first phrase of example 2 has no translation value. It is often omitted in spoken informal French.

  – 'ordering', 'forbidding', 'allowing'

ordonner que	*to order that* → 3
défendre que	*to forbid that* → 4
permettre que	*to allow that* → 5

  – opinion, expressing uncertainty

croire que	
penser que	*to think that* → 6
douter que	*to doubt that* → 7

  – emotion (e.g. regret, shame, pleasure)
  regretter que *to be sorry that* → 8
  être content/surpris *etc* **que** *to be pleased/surprised etc that* → 9

♦ After a superlative → 10

♦ After certain adjectives expressing some sort of 'uniqueness'

dernier ... qui/que	*last ... who/that*	
premier ... qui/que	*first ... who/that*	→ 11
meilleur ... qui/que	*best ... who/that*	
seul		
unique }**... qui/que**	*only ... who/that*	

1 **Nous voulons qu'elle soit contente**
   We want her to be happy *(literally: We want that she is happy)*
   Désirez-vous que je le fasse?
   Do you want me to do it?

2 **Il craint qu'il ne soit trop tard**
   He's afraid it may be too late
   Avez-vous peur qu'il ne revienne pas?
   Are you afraid that he won't come back?

3 **Il a ordonné qu'ils soient désormais à l'heure**
   He has ordered that they be on time from now on

4 **Elle défend que vous disiez cela**
   She forbids you to say that

5 **Permettez que nous vous aidions**
   Allow us to help you

6 **Je ne pense pas qu'ils soient venus**
   I don't think they came

7 **Nous doutons qu'il ait dit la vérité**
   We doubt that he told the truth

8 **Je regrette que vous ne puissiez pas venir**
   I'm sorry that you cannot come

9 **Je suis content que vous les aimiez**
   I'm pleased that you like them

10 **la personne la plus sympathique que je connaisse**
   the nicest person I know
   l'article le moins cher que j'aie jamais acheté
   the cheapest item I have ever bought

11 **Voici la dernière lettre qu'elle m'ait écrite**
   This is the last letter she wrote to me
   David est la seule personne qui puisse me conseiller
   David is the only person who can advise me

□ **The Subjunctive: when to use it** *(Continued)*

- After **si (...) que** *however* → ①
         qui que *whoever* → ②
         quoi que *whatever* → ③

- After **que** in the following:
  – to form the 3rd person imperative or to express a wish → ④
  – when **que** has the meaning *if*, replacing **si** in a clause → ⑤
  – when **que** has the meaning *whether* → ⑥

- In relative clauses following certain types of indefinite and negative construction → ⑦/⑧

- In set expressions → ⑨

1. **si courageux qu'il soit**
   however brave he may be
   si peu que ce soit
   however little it is

2. **Qui que vous soyez, allez-vous-en!**
   Whoever you are, go away!

3. **Quoi que nous fassions, ...**
   Whatever we do, ...

4. **Qu'il entre!**
   Let him come in!
   Que cela vous serve de leçon!
   Let that be a lesson to you!

5. **S'il fait beau et que tu te sentes mieux, nous irons ...**
   If it's nice and you're feeling better, we'll go ...

6. **Que tu viennes ou non, je ...**
   Whether you come or not, I ...

7. **Il cherche une maison qui ait deux caves**
   He's looking for a house which has two cellars
   (subjunctive used since such a house may or may not exist)
   J'ai besoin d'un livre qui décrive l'art du mime
   I need a book which describes the art of mime
   (subjunctive used since such a book may or may not exist)

8. **Je n'ai rencontré personne qui la connaisse**
   I haven't met anyone who knows her
   Il n'y a rien qui puisse vous empêcher de ...
   There's nothing that can prevent you from ...

9. **Vive le roi!**
   Long live the king!
   Que Dieu vous bénisse!
   God bless you!

❑ Verbs governing à and de

The following lists (pp 64 to 72) contain common verbal constructions using the prepositions **à** and **de**

Note the following abbreviations:

infin.	infinitive	**qn**	quelqu'un
perf. infin.	perfect infinitive*	*sb*	somebody
qch	quelque chose	*sth*	something

*For formation see p 46

accuser qn de qch/de + perf. infin.	*to accuse sb of sth/of doing, having done* → 1
accoutumer qn à qch/à + infin.	*to accustom sb to sth/to doing*
acheter qch à qn	*to buy sth from sb/for sb* → 2
achever de + infin.	*to end up doing*
aider qn à + infin.	*to help sb to do* → 3
s'amuser à + infin.	*to have fun doing*
s'apercevoir de qch	*to notice sth* → 4
apprendre qch à qn	*to teach sb sth*
apprendre à + infin.	*to learn to do* → 5
apprendre à qn à + infin.	*to teach sb to do* → 6
s'approcher de qn/qch	*to approach sb/sth* → 7
arracher qch à qn	*to snatch sth from sb* → 8
(s')arrêter de + infin.	*to stop doing* → 9
arriver à + infin.	*to manage to do* → 10
assister à qch	*to attend sth, be at sth*
s'attendre à + infin.	*to expect to do* → 11
blâmer qn de qch/de + perf. infin.	*to blame sb for sth/for having done* → 12
cacher qch à qn	*to hide sth from sb* → 13
cesser de + infin.	*to stop doing* → 14

1. **Il m'a accusé d'avoir menti**
   He accused me of lying

2. **Marie-Christine leur a acheté deux billets**
   Marie-Christine bought two tickets from/for them

3. **Aidez-moi à porter ces valises**
   Help me to carry these cases

4. **Il ne s'est pas aperçu de son erreur**
   He didn't notice his mistake

5. **Elle apprend à lire**
   She's learning to read

6. **Je lui apprends à nager**
   I'm teaching him/her to swim

7. **Elle s'est approchée de moi, en disant '...'**
   She came up to me, saying '...'

8. **Le voleur lui a arraché l'argent**
   The thief snatched the money from him/her

9. **Arrêtez de faire du bruit!**
   Stop being (so) noisy!

10. **Je n'arrive pas à le comprendre**
    I can't understand it

11. **Est-ce qu'elle s'attendait à le voir?**
    Was she expecting to see him?

12. **Je ne la blâme pas de l'avoir fait**
    I don't blame her for doing it

13. **Cache-les-leur!**
    Hide them from them!

14. **Est-ce qu'il a cessé de pleuvoir?**
    Has it stopped raining?

❑ Verbs governing à and de *(Continued)*

changer de qch	*to change sth* → 1
se charger de qch/de + infin.	*to see to sth/undertake to do*
chercher à + infin.	*to try to do*
commander à qn **de** + infin.	*to order sb to do* → 2
commencer à/de + infin.	*to begin to do* → 3
conseiller à qn **de** + infin.	*to advise sb to do* → 4
consentir à qch/**à** + infin.	*to agree to sth/to do* → 5
continuer à/de + infin.	*to continue to do*
craindre de + infin.	*to be afraid to do/of doing*
décider de + infin.	*to decide to* → 6
se décider à + infin.	*to make up one's mind to do*
défendre à qn **de** + infin.	*to forbid sb to do* → 7
demander qch **à** qn	*to ask sb sth/for sth* → 8
demander à qn **de** + infin.	*to ask sb to do* → 9
se dépêcher de + infin.	*to hurry to do*
dépendre de qn/qch	*to depend on sb/sth*
déplaire à qn	*to displease sb* → 10
désobéir à qn	*to disobey sb* → 11
dire à qn **de** + infin.	*to tell sb to do* → 12
dissuader qn **de** + infin.	*to dissuade sb from doing*
douter de qch	*to doubt sth*
se douter de qch	*to suspect sth*
s'efforcer de + infin.	*to strive to do*
empêcher qn **de** + infin.	*to prevent sb from doing* → 13
emprunter qch **à** qn	*to borrow sth from sb* → 14
encourager qn **à** + infin.	*to encourage sb to do* → 15
enlever qch **à** qn	*to take sth away from sb*
enseigner qch **à** qn	*to teach sb sth*
enseigner à qn **à** + infin.	*to teach sb to do*
entreprendre de + infin.	*to undertake to do*
essayer de + infin.	*to try to do* → 16
éviter de + infin.	*to avoid doing* → 17

1. **J'ai changé d'avis/de robe**
   I changed my mind/my dress
   Il faut changer de train à Toulouse
   You have to change trains at Toulouse

2. **Il leur a commandé de tirer**
   He ordered them to shoot

3. **Il commence à neiger**
   It's starting to snow

4. **Il leur a conseillé d'attendre**
   He advised them to wait

5. **Je n'ai pas consenti à l'aider**
   I haven't agreed to help him/her

6. **Qu'est-ce que vous avez décidé de faire?**
   What have you decided to do?

7. **Je leur ai défendu de sortir**
   I've forbidden them to go out

8. **Je lui ai demandé l'heure**
   I asked him/her the time
   Il lui a demandé un livre
   He asked him/her for a book

9. **Demande à Alain de le faire**
   Ask Alan to do it

10. **Leur attitude lui déplaît**
    He/She doesn't like their attitude

11. **Ils lui désobéissent souvent**
    They often disobey him/her

12. **Dites-leur de se taire**
    Tell them to be quiet

13. **Le bruit m'empêche de travailler**
    The noise is preventing me from working

14. **Puis-je vous emprunter ce stylo?**
    May I borrow this pen from you?

15. **Elle encourage ses enfants à être indépendants**
    She encourages her children to be independent

16. **Essayez d'arriver à l'heure**
    Try to arrive on time

17. **Il évite de lui parler**
    He avoids speaking to him/her

◻ Verbs governing à and de *(Continued)*

s'excuser de qch/de + (perf.) infin.	*to apologize for sth/for doing, having done* → ⓵
exceller à + infin.	*to excel at doing*
se fâcher de qch	*to be annoyed at sth*
feindre de + infin.	*to pretend to do* → ⓶
féliciter qn de qch/de + (perf.) infin.	*to congratulate sb on sth/on doing, having done* → ⓷
se fier à qn	*to trust sb* → ⓸
finir de + infin.	*to finish doing* → ⓹
forcer qn à + infin.	*to force sb to do*
habituer qn à + infin.	*to accustom sb to doing*
s'habituer à + infin.	*to get/be used to doing* → ⓺
se hâter de + infin.	*to hurry to do*
hésiter à + infin.	*to hesitate to do*
interdire à qn de + infin.	*to forbid sb to do* → ⓻
s'intéresser à qn/qch/à + infin.	*to be interested in sb/sth/in doing* → ⓼
inviter qn à + infin.	*to invite sb to do* → ⓽
jouer à (+ sports, games)	*to play* → ⓾
jouer de (+ musical instruments)	*to play* → ⑪
jouir de qch	*to enjoy sth* → ⑫
jurer de + infin.	*to swear to do*
louer qn de qch	*to praise sb for sth*
manquer à qn	*to be missed by sb* → ⑬
manquer de qch	*to lack sth*
manquer de + infin.	*to fail to do* → ⑭
se marier à qn	*to marry sb*
se méfier de qn	*to distrust sb*
menacer de + infin.	*to threaten to do* → ⑮
mériter de + infin.	*to deserve to do* → ⑯
se mettre à + infin.	*to begin to do*
se moquer de qn/qch	*to make fun of sb/sth*
négliger de + infin.	*to fail to do*

1. **Je m'excuse d'être (arrivé) en retard**
   I apologize for being/arriving late

2. **Elle feint de dormir**
   She's pretending to be asleep

3. **Je l'ai félicitée d'avoir gagné**
   I congratulated her on winning

4. **Je ne me fie pas à ces gens-là**
   I don't trust those people

5. **Avez-vous fini de lire ce journal?**
   Have you finished reading this newspaper?

6. **Il s'est habitué à boire moins de café**
   He got used to drinking less coffee

7. **Il a interdit aux enfants de jouer avec des allumettes**
   He's forbidden the children to play with matches

8. **Elle s'intéresse beaucoup au sport**
   She's very interested in sport

9. **Il m'a invitée à danser**
   He asked me to dance

10. **Elle joue au tennis et au hockey**
    She plays tennis and hockey

11. **Il joue du piano et de la guitare**
    He plays the piano and the guitar

12. **Il jouit d'une santé solide**
    He enjoys good health

13. **Tu manques à tes parents**
    Your parents miss you

14. **Je ne manquerai pas de le lui dire**
    I'll be sure to tell him/her about it

15. **Elle a menacé de démissionner tout de suite**
    She threatened to resign at once

16. **Ils méritent d'être promus**
    They deserve to be promoted

☐ Verbs governing à and de *(Continued)*

nuire à qch	to harm sth → 1
obéir à qn	to obey sb
obliger qn à + infin.	to oblige sb to do → 2
s'occuper de qch/qn	to look after sth/sb → 3
offrir de + infin.	to offer to do → 4
omettre de + infin.	to fail to do
ordonner à qn de + infin.	to order sb to do → 5
ôter qch à qn	to take sth away from sb
oublier de + infin.	to forget to do
pardonner qch à qn	to forgive sb for sth
pardonner à qn de + perf. infin.	to forgive sb for having done → 6
parvenir à + infin.	to manage to do
se passer de qch	to do/go without sth → 7
penser à qn/qch	to think about sb/sth → 8
permettre qch à qn	to allow sb sth
permettre à qn de + infin.	to allow sb to do → 9
persister à + infin.	to persist in doing
persuader qn à + infin.	to persuade sb to do → 10
se plaindre de qch	to complain about sth
plaire à qn	to please sb → 11
pousser qn à + infin.	to urge sb to do
prendre qch à qn	to take sth from sb → 12
préparer qn à + infin.	to prepare sb to do
se préparer à + infin.	to get ready to do
prier qn de + infin.	to beg sb to do
profiter de qch/de + infin.	to take advantage of sth/of doing
promettre à qn de + infin.	to promise sb to do → 13
proposer de + infin.	to suggest doing → 14
punir qn de qch	to punish sb for sth → 15
récompenser qn de qch	to reward sb for sth
réfléchir à qch	to think about sth
refuser de + infin.	to refuse to do → 16

1. **Ce mode de vie va nuire à sa santé**
   This lifestyle will damage her health

2. **Il les a obligés à faire la vaisselle**
   He made them do the washing-up

3. **Je m'occupe de ma nièce**
   I'm looking after my niece

4. **Stuart a offert de nous accompagner**
   Stuart has offered to go with us

5. **Les soldats leur ont ordonné de se rendre**
   The soldiers ordered them to give themselves up

6. **Est-ce que tu as pardonné à Charles de t'avoir menti?**
   Have you forgiven Charles for lying to you?

7. **Nous nous sommes passés d'électricité pendant plusieurs jours**
   We did without electricity for several days

8. **Je pense souvent à toi**
   I often think about you

9. **Permettez-moi de continuer, s'il vous plaît**
   Allow me to go on, please

10. **Elle nous a persuadés de rester**
    She persuaded us to stay

11. **Est-ce que ce genre de film lui plaît?**
    Does he/she like this kind of film?

12. **Je lui ai pris son baladeur**
    I took his personal stereo from him

13. **Ils ont promis à Pascale de venir**
    They promised Pascale that they would come

14. **J'ai proposé de les inviter**
    I suggested inviting them

15. **Il a été puni de sa malhonnêteté**
    He has been punished for his dishonesty

16. **Il a refusé de coopérer**
    He has refused to cooperate

□ **Verbs governing à and de** *(Continued)*

regretter de + perf. infin.	*to regret doing, having done* → 1
remercier qn de qch/de + perf. infin.	*to thank sb for sth/for doing, having done* → 2
renoncer à qch/à + infin.	*to give sth up/give up doing*
reprocher qch à qn	*to reproach sb with/for sth* → 3
résister à qch	*to resist sth* → 4
résoudre de + infin.	*to resolve to do*
ressembler à qn/qch	*to look/be like sb/sth* → 5
réussir à + infin.	*to manage to do* → 6
rire de qn/qch	*to laugh at sb/sth*
risquer de + infin.	*to risk doing* → 7
servir à qch/à + infin.	*to be used for sth/for doing* → 8
se servir de qch	*to use sth; to help oneself to sth* → 9
songer à + infin.	*to think of doing*
se souvenir de qn/qch/de + perf. infin.	*to remember sb/sth/doing, having done* → 10
succéder à qn	*to succeed sb*
survivre à qn	*to outlive sb* → 11
tâcher de + infin.	*to try to do* → 12
tarder à + infin.	*to delay doing* → 13
tendre à + infin.	*to tend to do*
tenir à + infin.	*to be keen to do* → 14
tenter de + infin.	*to try to do* → 15
se tromper de qch	*to be wrong about sth* → 16
venir de* + infin.	*to have just done* → 17
vivre de qch	*to live on sth*
voler qch à qn	*to steal sth from sb*

*See also Use of Tenses, pp 54 and 56

1. **Je regrette de ne pas vous avoir écrit plus tôt**
I'm sorry for not writing to you sooner

2. **Nous les avons remerciés de leur gentillesse**
We thanked them for their kindness

3. **On lui reproche son manque d'enthousiasme**
They're reproaching him for his lack of enthusiasm

4. **Comment résistez-vous à la tentation?**
How do you resist temptation?

5. **Elles ressemblent beaucoup à leur mère**
They look very like their mother

6. **Vous avez réussi à me convaincre**
You've managed to convince me

7. **Vous risquez de tomber en faisant cela**
You risk falling doing that

8. **Ce bouton sert à régler le volume**
This knob is (used) for adjusting the volume

9. **Il s'est servi d'un tournevis pour l'ouvrir**
He used a screwdriver to open it

10. **Vous vous souvenez de Lucienne?**
Do you remember Lucienne?
Il ne se souvient pas de l'avoir perdu
He doesn't remember losing it

11. **Elle a survécu à son mari**
She outlived her husband

12. **Tâchez de ne pas être en retard!**
Try not to be late!

13. **Il n'a pas tardé à prendre une décision**
He was not long in taking a decision

14. **Elle tient à le faire elle-même**
She's keen to do it herself

15. **J'ai tenté de la comprendre**
I've tried to understand her

16. **Je me suis trompé de route**
I took the wrong road

17. **Mon père vient de téléphoner**   **Nous venions d'arriver**
My father's just phoned   We had just arrived

◻ Irregular Verbs

The verbs listed opposite and conjugated on pp 76 to 131 provide the main patterns for irregular verbs. The verbs are grouped opposite according to their infinitive ending (except **avoir** and **être**), and are shown in the following tables in alphabetical order.

In the tables, the most important irregular verbs are given in their most common simple tenses, together with the imperative and the present participle.

The auxiliary (**avoir** or **être**) is also shown for each verb, together with the past participle, to enable you to form all the compound tenses, as on pp 24 and 26.

• For a fuller list of irregular verbs, the reader is referred to Collins Gem French Verb Tables, which shows you how to conjugate some 2000 French verbs.

avoir
       être

'-er':	aller	**'-re':**	battre
	envoyer		boire
			connaître
'-ir':	acquérir		coudre
	bouillir		craindre
	courir		croire
	cueillir		croître
	dormir		cuire
	fuir		dire
	haïr		écrire
	mourir		faire
	ouvrir		lire
	partir		mettre
	sentir		moudre
	servir		naître
	sortir		paraître
	tenir		plaire
	venir		prendre
	vêtir		résoudre
			rire
'-oir':	s'asseoir		rompre
	devoir		suffire
	falloir		suivre
	pleuvoir		se taire
	pouvoir		vaincre
	recevoir		vivre
	savoir		
	valoir		
	voir		
	vouloir		

acquérir *to acquire*	Auxiliary: **avoir**

PAST PARTICIPLE	IMPERATIVE
acquis	**acquiers**
	acquérons
PRESENT PARTICIPLE	**acquérez**
acquérant	

PRESENT	IMPERFECT
j'acquiers	j'acquérais
tu acquiers	tu acquérais
il acquiert	il acquérait
nous acquérons	nous acquérions
vous acquérez	vous acquériez
ils acquierent	ils acquéraient

FUTURE	CONDITIONAL
j'acquerrai	j'acquerrais
tu acquerras	tu acquerrais
il acquerra	il acquerrait
nous acquerrons	nous acquerrions
vous acquerrez	vous acquerriez
ils acquerront	ils acquerraient

PRESENT SUBJUNCTIVE	PAST HISTORIC
j'acquière	j'acquis
tu acquières	tu acquis
il acquière	il acquit
nous acquérions	nous acquîmes
vous acquériez	vous acquîtes
ils acquièrent	ils acquirent

aller *to go*	Auxiliary: **être**

PAST PARTICIPLE	IMPERATIVE
allé	**va**
	allons
PRESENT PARTICIPLE	allez
allant	

PRESENT		IMPERFECT	
je	**vais**		j'allais
tu	**vas**	tu	allais
il	**va**	il	allait
nous	allons	nous	allions
vous	allez	vous	alliez
ils	**vont**	ils	allaient

FUTURE		CONDITIONAL	
	j'irai		**j'irais**
tu	**iras**	**tu**	**irais**
il	**ira**	**il**	**irait**
nous	**Irons**	**nous**	**irions**
vous	**irez**	**vous**	**iriez**
ils	**iront**	**ils**	**iraient**

PRESENT SUBJUNCTIVE		PAST HISTORIC	
	j'aille		j'allai
tu	**ailles**	tu	allas
il	**aille**	il	alla
nous	allions	nous	allâmes
vous	alliez	vous	allâtes
ils	**aillent**	ils	allèrent

s'asseoir *to sit down*	Auxiliary: **être**

PAST PARTICIPLE	IMPERATIVE
assis	assieds-toi
	asseyons-nous
PRESENT PARTICIPLE	asseyez-vous
s'asseyant	

PRESENT	IMPERFECT
je m'assieds *or* assois	je m'asseyais
tu t'assieds *or* assois	tu t'asseyais
il s'assied *or* assoit	il s'asseyait
nous nous asseyons *or* assoyons	nous nous asseyions
vous vous asseyez *or* assoyez	vous vous asseyiez
ils s'asseyent *or* assoient	ils s'asseyaient

FUTURE	CONDITIONAL
je m'assiérai	je m'assiérais
tu t'assiéras	tu t'assiérais
il s'assiéra	il s'assiérait
nous nous assiérons	nous nous assiérions
vous vous assiérez	vous vous assiériez
ils s'assiéront	ils s'assiéraient

PRESENT SUBJUNCTIVE	PAST HISTORIC
je m'asseye	je m'assis
tu t'asseyes	tu t'assis
il s'asseye	il s'assit
nous nous asseyions	nous nous assîmes
vous vous asseyiez	vous vous assîtes
ils s'asseyent	ils s'assirent

avoir to have	Auxiliary: **avoir**

PAST PARTICIPLE	IMPERATIVE
eu	aie
	ayons
	ayez
PRESENT PARTICIPLE	
ayant	

PRESENT	IMPERFECT
j'ai	j'avais
tu as	tu avais
il a	il avait
nous avons	nous avions
vous avez	vous aviez
ils ont	ils avaient

FUTURE	CONDITIONAL
j'aurai	j'aurais
tu auras	tu aurais
il aura	il aurait
nous aurons	nous aurions
vous aurez	vous auriez
ils auront	ils auraient

PRESENT SUBJUNCTIVE	PAST HISTORIC
j'aie	j'eus
tu aies	tu eus
il ait	il eut
nous ayons	nous eûmes
vous ayez	vous eûtes
ils aient	ils eurent

battre to beat	Auxiliary: **avoir**

PAST PARTICIPLE	IMPERATIVE
battu	**bats**
	battons
PRESENT PARTICIPLE	battez
battant	

PRESENT	IMPERFECT
je **bats**	je battais
tu **bats**	tu battais
il **bat**	il battait
nous battons	nous battions
vous battez	vous battiez
ils battent	ils battaient

FUTURE	CONDITIONAL
je battrai	je battrais
tu battras	tu battrais
il battra	il battrait
nous battrons	nous battrions
vous battrez	vous battriez
ils battront	ils battraient

PRESENT SUBJUNCTIVE	PAST HISTORIC
je batte	je battis
tu battes	tu battis
il batte	il battit
nous battions	nous battîmes
vous battiez	vous battîtes
ils battent	ils battirent

grammar

| **boire** *to drink* | Auxiliary: **avoir** |

PAST PARTICIPLE

bu

PRESENT PARTICIPLE

buvant

IMPERATIVE

bois
buvons
buvez

PRESENT	IMPERFECT
je bois	je **buvais**
tu bois	tu **buvais**
il boit	il **buvait**
nous **buvons**	**nous** **buvions**
vous **buvez**	**vous** **buviez**
ils **boivent**	**ils** **buvaient**

FUTURE	CONDITIONAL
je boirai	je boirais
tu boiras	tu boirais
il boira	il boirait
nous boirons	nous boirions
vous boirez	vous boiriez
ils boiront	ils boiraient

PRESENT SUBJUNCTIVE	PAST HISTORIC
je boive	**je bus**
tu boives	**tu bus**
il boive	**il but**
nous **buvions**	**nous** **bûmes**
vous **buviez**	**vous** **bûtes**
ils **boivent**	**ils** **burent**

bouillir *to boil*	Auxiliary: **avoir**

PAST PARTICIPLE

bouilli

PRESENT PARTICIPLE

bouillant

IMPERATIVE

bous
bouillons
bouillez

PRESENT	IMPERFECT
je bous	**je bouillais**
tu bous	**tu bouillais**
il bout	**il bouillait**
nous bouillons	**nous bouillions**
vous bouillez	**vous bouilliez**
ils bouillent	**ils bouillaient**

FUTURE	CONDITIONAL
je bouillirai	je bouillirais
tu bouilliras	tu bouillirais
il bouillira	il bouillirait
nous bouillirons	nous bouillirions
vous bouillirez	vous bouilliriez
ils bouilliront	ils bouilliraient

PRESENT SUBJUNCTIVE	PAST HISTORIC
je bouille	je bouillis
tu bouilles	tu bouillis
il bouille	il bouillit
nous bouillions	nous bouillîmes
vous bouilliez	vous bouillîtes
ils bouillent	ils bouillirent

connaître *to know*	Auxiliary: **avoir**

PAST PARTICIPLE

connu

PRESENT PARTICIPLE

connaissant

IMPERATIVE

connais
connaissons
connaissez

PRESENT	IMPERFECT
je connais	je connaissais
tu connais	tu connaissais
il connaît	il connaissait
nous connaissons	nous connaissions
vous connaissez	vous connaissiez
ils connaissent	ils connaissaient

FUTURE	CONDITIONAL
je connaîtrai	je connaîtrais
tu connaîtras	tu connaîtrais
il connaîtra	il connaîtrait
nous connaîtrons	nous connaîtrions
vous connaîtrez	vous connaîtriez
ils connaîtront	ils connaîtraient

PRESENT SUBJUNCTIVE	PAST HISTORIC
je connaisse	je connus
tu connaisses	tu connus
il connaisse	il connut
nous connaissions	nous connûmes
vous connaissiez	vous connûtes
ils connaissent	ils connurent

coudre to sew	Auxiliary: **avoir**

PAST PARTICIPLE	IMPERATIVE
cousu	couds
	cousons
	cousez
PRESENT PARTICIPLE	
cousant	

PRESENT	IMPERFECT
je couds	**je cousais**
tu couds	**tu cousais**
il coud	**il cousait**
nous cousons	**nous cousions**
vous cousez	**vous cousiez**
ils cousent	**ils cousaient**

FUTURE	CONDITIONAL
je coudrai	je coudrais
tu coudras	tu coudrais
il coudra	il coudrait
nous coudrons	nous coudrions
vous coudrez	vous coudriez
ils coudront	ils coudraient

PRESENT SUBJUNCTIVE	PAST HISTORIC
je couse	**je cousis**
tu couses	**tu cousis**
il couse	**il cousit**
nous cousions	**nous cousîmes**
vous cousiez	**vous cousîtes**
ils cousent	**ils cousirent**

courir *to run*	Auxiliary: **avoir**

PAST PARTICIPLE	IMPERATIVE
couru	cours
	courons
	courez
PRESENT PARTICIPLE	
courant	

PRESENT		IMPERFECT	
je	cours	je	courais
tu	cours	tu	courais
il	court	il	courait
nous	courons	nous	courions
vous	courez	vous	couriez
ils	courent	ils	couraient

FUTURE		CONDITIONAL	
je	courrai	je	courrais
tu	courras	tu	courrais
il	courra	il	courrait
nous	courrons	nous	courrions
vous	courrez	vous	courriez
ils	courront	ils	courraient

PRESENT SUBJUNCTIVE		PAST HISTORIC	
je	coure	je	courus
tu	coures	tu	courus
il	coure	il	courut
nous	courions	nous	courûmes
vous	couriez	vous	courûtes
ils	courent	ils	coururent

craindre to fear	Auxiliary: **avoir**

PAST PARTICIPLE	IMPERATIVE
craint	crains
	craignons
PRESENT PARTICIPLE	craignez
craignant	

PRESENT	IMPERFECT
je **crains**	je **craignais**
tu **crains**	tu **craignais**
il **craint**	il **craignait**
nous **craignons**	nous **craignions**
vous **craignez**	vous **craigniez**
ils **craignent**	ils **craignaient**

FUTURE	CONDITIONAL
je craindrai	je craindrais
tu craindras	tu craindrais
il craindra	il craindrait
nous craindrons	nous craindrions
vous craindrez	vous craindriez
ils craindront	ils craindraient

PRESENT SUBJUNCTIVE	PAST HISTORIC
je **craigne**	je **craignis**
tu **craignes**	tu **craignis**
il **craigne**	il **craignit**
nous **craignions**	nous **craignîmes**
vous **craigniez**	vous **craignîtes**
ils **craignent**	ils **craignirent**

Verbs ending in **-eindre** and **-oindre** are conjugated similarly

croire *to believe*	Auxiliary: **avoir**

PAST PARTICIPLE	IMPERATIVE
cru	crois
	croyons
	croyez
PRESENT PARTICIPLE	
croyant	

PRESENT		IMPERFECT	
je	crois	**je**	**croyais**
tu	crois	**tu**	**croyais**
il	**croit**	il	croyait
nous	**croyons**	nous	croyions
vous	**croyez**	vous	croyiez
ils	croient	**ils**	**croyaient**

FUTURE		CONDITIONAL	
je	croirai	je	croirais
tu	croiras	tu	croirais
il	croira	il	croirait
nous	croirons	nous	croirions
vous	croirez	vous	croiriez
ils	croiront	ils	croiraient

PRESENT SUBJUNCTIVE		PAST HISTORIC	
je	croie	**je**	**crus**
tu	croies	**tu**	**crus**
il	croie	**il**	**crut**
nous	**croyions**	nous	crûmes
vous	**croyiez**	vous	crûtes
ils	croient	**ils**	**crurent**

croître to grow	Auxiliary: **avoir**

PAST PARTICIPLE

crû

PRESENT PARTICIPLE

croissant

IMPERATIVE

crois
croissons
croissez

PRESENT	IMPERFECT
je **crois**	je **croissais**
tu **crois**	tu **croissais**
il croît	il **croissait**
nous **croissons**	nous **croissions**
vous **croissez**	vous **croissiez**
ils **croissent**	ils **croissaient**

FUTURE	CONDITIONAL
je croîtrai	je croîtrais
tu croîtras	tu croîtrais
il croîtra	il croîtrait
nous croîtrons	nous croîtrions
vous croîtrez	vous croîtriez
ils croîtront	ils croîtraient

PRESENT SUBJUNCTIVE	PAST HISTORIC
je **croisse**	je **crûs**
tu **croisses**	tu **crûs**
il **croisse**	il **crût**
nous **croissions**	nous **crûmes**
vous **croissiez**	vous **crûtes**
ils **croissent**	ils **crûrent**

cueillir *to pick*	Auxiliary: **avoir**

PAST PARTICIPLE

cueilli

PRESENT PARTICIPLE

cueillant

IMPERATIVE

cueille
cueillons
cueillez

PRESENT	IMPERFECT
je **cueille**	je **cueillais**
tu **cueilles**	tu **cueillais**
il **cueille**	il **cueillait**
nous **cueillons**	nous **cueillions**
vous **cueillez**	vous **cueilliez**
ils **cueillent**	ils **cueillaient**

FUTURE	CONDITIONAL
je **cueillerai**	je **cueillerais**
tu **cueilleras**	tu **cueillerais**
il **cueillera**	il **cueillerait**
nous **cueillerons**	nous **cueillerions**
vous **cueillerez**	vous **cueilleriez**
ils **cueilleront**	ils **cueilleraient**

PRESENT SUBJUNCTIVE	PAST HISTORIC
je **cueille**	je cueillis
tu **cueilles**	tu cueillis
il **cueille**	il cueillit
nous **cueillions**	nous cueillîmes
vous **cueilliez**	vous cueillîtes
ils **cueillent**	ils cueillirent

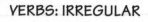

cuire *to cook*	Auxiliary: **avoir**

PAST PARTICIPLE

cuit

IMPERATIVE

cuis
cuisons
cuisez

PRESENT PARTICIPLE

cuisant

PRESENT	IMPERFECT
je cuis	**je cuisais**
tu cuis	**tu cuisais**
il cuit	il cuisait
nous cuisons	nous cuisions
vous cuisez	vous cuisiez
ils cuisent	ils cuisaient

FUTURE	CONDITIONAL
je cuirai	je cuirais
tu cuiras	tu cuirais
il cuira	il cuirait
nous cuirons	nous cuirions
vous cuirez	vous cuiriez
ils cuiront	ils cuiraient

PRESENT SUBJUNCTIVE	PAST HISTORIC
je cuise	**je cuisis**
tu cuises	**tu cuisis**
il cuise	**il cuisit**
nous cuisions	**nous cuisîmes**
vous cuisiez	**vous cuisîtes**
ils cuisent	**ils cuisirent**

nuire *to harm*, conjugated similarly, but past participle **nui**

devoir to have to; to owe	Auxiliary: **avoir**

PAST PARTICIPLE

dû, due

PRESENT PARTICIPLE

devant

IMPERATIVE

dois
devons
devez

PRESENT	IMPERFECT
je **dois**	je **devais**
tu **dois**	tu **devais**
il **doit**	il **devait**
nous **devons**	nous **devions**
vous **devez**	vous **deviez**
ils **doivent**	ils **devaient**

FUTURE	CONDITIONAL
je **devrai**	je **devrais**
tu **devras**	tu **devrais**
il **devra**	il **devrait**
nous **devrons**	nous **devrions**
vous **devrez**	vous **devriez**
ils **devront**	ils **devraient**

PRESENT SUBJUNCTIVE	PAST HISTORIC
je **doive**	je **dus**
tu **doives**	tu **dus**
il **doive**	il **dut**
nous **devions**	nous **dûmes**
vous **deviez**	vous **dûtes**
ils **doivent**	ils **durent**

dire _to say, tell_	Auxiliary: **avoir**

PAST PARTICIPLE	IMPERATIVE
dit	dis
	disons
	dites
PRESENT PARTICIPLE	
disant	

PRESENT	IMPERFECT
je **dis**	je **disais**
tu **dis**	tu **disais**
il **dit**	il **disait**
nous **disons**	nous **disions**
vous **dites**	vous **disiez**
ils **disent**	ils **disaient**

FUTURE	CONDITIONAL
je **dirai**	je **dirais**
tu **diras**	tu **dirais**
il **dira**	il **dirait**
nous **dirons**	nous **dirions**
vous **direz**	vous **diriez**
ils **diront**	ils **diraient**

PRESENT SUBJUNCTIVE	PAST HISTORIC
je **dise**	je **dis**
tu **dises**	tu **dis**
il **dise**	il **dit**
nous **disions**	nous **dîmes**
vous **disiez**	vous **dîtes**
ils **disent**	ils **dirent**

interdire _to forbid,_ conjugated similarly, but 2nd person plural of the present tense is **vous interdisez**

dormir *to sleep*	Auxiliary: **avoir**

PAST PARTICIPLE

dormi

PRESENT PARTICIPLE

dormant

IMPERATIVE

dors
dormons
dormez

PRESENT	IMPERFECT
je **dors**	je **dormais**
tu **dors**	tu **dormais**
il **dort**	il **dormait**
nous **dormons**	nous **dormions**
vous **dormez**	vous **dormiez**
ils **dorment**	ils **dormaient**

FUTURE	CONDITIONAL
je dormirai	je dormirais
tu dormiras	tu dormirais
il dormira	il dormirait
nous dormirons	nous dormirions
vous dormirez	vous dormiriez
ils dormiront	ils dormiraient

PRESENT SUBJUNCTIVE	PAST HISTORIC
je **dorme**	je dormis
tu **dormes**	tu dormis
il **dorme**	il dormit
nous **dormions**	nous dormîmes
vous **dormiez**	vous dormîtes
ils **dorment**	ils dormirent

écrire to write	Auxiliary: **avoir**

PAST PARTICIPLE	IMPERATIVE
écrit	écris
	écrivons
	écrivez
PRESENT PARTICIPLE	
écrivant	

PRESENT		IMPERFECT	
	j'écris		j'écrivais
tu	écris	**tu**	**écrivais**
il	écrit	il	écrivait
nous	**écrivons**	**nous**	**écrivions**
vous	**écrivez**	**vous**	**écriviez**
ils	**écrivent**	**ils**	**écrivaient**

FUTURE		CONDITIONAL	
	j'écrirai		j'écrirais
tu	écriras	tu	écrirais
il	écrira	il	écrirait
nous	écrirons	nous	écririons
vous	écrirez	vous	écririez
ils	écriront	ils	écriraient

PRESENT SUBJUNCTIVE		PAST HISTORIC	
	j'écrive		**j'écrivis**
tu	**écrives**	**tu**	**écrivis**
il	**écrive**	**il**	**écrivit**
nous	**écrivions**	**nous**	**écrivîmes**
vous	**écriviez**	**vous**	**écrivîtes**
ils	**écrivent**	**ils**	**écrivirent**

envoyer _to send_	Auxiliary: **avoir**

PAST PARTICIPLE	IMPERATIVE
envoyé	envoie
	envoyons
PRESENT PARTICIPLE	envoyez
envoyant	

PRESENT	IMPERFECT
j'envoie	j'envoyais
tu envoies	tu envoyais
il envoie	il envoyait
nous envoyons	nous envoyions
vous envoyez	vous envoyiez
ils envoient	ils envoyaient

FUTURE	CONDITIONAL
j'enverrai	**j'enverrais**
tu enverras	**tu enverrais**
il enverra	**il enverrait**
nous enverrons	**nous enverrions**
vous enverrez	**vous enverriez**
ils enverront	**ils enverraient**

PRESENT SUBJUNCTIVE	PAST HISTORIC
j'envoie	j'envoyai
tu envoies	tu envoyas
il envoie	il envoya
nous envoyions	nous envoyâmes
vous envoyiez	vous envoyâtes
ils envoient	ils envoyèrent

être *to be*	Auxiliary: **avoir**

PAST PARTICIPLE	IMPERATIVE
été	sois
	soyons
	soyez
PRESENT PARTICIPLE	
étant	

PRESENT	IMPERFECT
je suis	j'étais
tu es	tu étais
il est	il était
nous sommes	nous étions
vous êtes	vous étiez
ils sont	ils étaient

FUTURE	CONDITIONAL
je serai	je serais
tu seras	tu serais
il sera	il serait
nous serons	nous serions
vous serez	vous seriez
ils seront	ils seraient

PRESENT SUBJUNCTIVE	PAST HISTORIC
je sois	je fus
tu sois	tu fus
il soit	il fut
nous soyons	nous fûmes
vous soyez	vous fûtes
ils soient	ils furent

faire *to do; to make*	Auxiliary: **avoir**

PAST PARTICIPLE

fait

IMPERATIVE

fais
faisons
faites

PRESENT PARTICIPLE

faisant

PRESENT	IMPERFECT
je fais	je faisais
tu fais	tu faisais
il fait	il faisait
nous faisons	nous faisions
vous faites	vous faisiez
ils font	ils faisaient

FUTURE	CONDITIONAL
je ferai	je ferais
tu feras	tu ferais
il fera	il ferait
nous ferons	nous ferions
vous ferez	vous feriez
ils feront	ils feraient

PRESENT SUBJUNCTIVE	PAST HISTORIC
je fasse	je fis
tu fasses	tu fis
il fasse	il fit
nous fassions	nous fîmes
vous fassiez	vous fîtes
ils fassent	ils firent

falloir *to be necessary* | Auxiliary: **avoir**

PAST PARTICIPLE

fallu

IMPERATIVE

not used

PRESENT PARTICIPLE

not used

PRESENT	IMPERFECT
il **faut**	il **fallait**

FUTURE	CONDITIONAL
il **faudra**	il **faudrait**

PRESENT SUBJUNCTIVE	PAST HISTORIC
il **faille**	il **fallut**

fuir *to flee*	Auxiliary: **avoir**

PAST PARTICIPLE	IMPERATIVE
fui	fuis
	fuyons
	fuyez
PRESENT PARTICIPLE	
fuyant	

PRESENT	IMPERFECT
je fuis	je **fuyais**
tu fuis	tu **fuyais**
il fuit	il **fuyait**
nous fuyons	**nous fuyions**
vous fuyez	**vous fuyiez**
ils fuient	**ils fuyaient**

FUTURE	CONDITIONAL
je fuirai	je fuirais
tu fuiras	tu fuirais
il fuira	il fuirait
nous fuirons	nous fuirions
vous fuirez	vous fuiriez
ils fuiront	ils fuiraient

PRESENT SUBJUNCTIVE	PAST HISTORIC
je fuie	je fuis
tu fuies	tu fuis
il fuie	il fuit
nous fuyions	nous fuîmes
vous fuyiez	vous fuîtes
ils fuient	ils fuirent

haïr *to hate*	Auxiliary: **avoir**

PAST PARTICIPLE	IMPERATIVE
haï	hais
	haïssons
	haïssez
PRESENT PARTICIPLE	
haïssant	

PRESENT	IMPERFECT
je hais	**je haïssais**
tu hais	**tu haïssais**
il hait	**il haïssait**
nous haïssons	**nous haïssions**
vous haïssez	**vous haïssiez**
ils haïssent	**ils haïssaient**

FUTURE	CONDITIONAL
je haïrai	je haïrais
tu haïras	tu haïrais
il haïra	il haïrait
nous haïrons	nous haïrions
vous haïrez	vous haïriez
ils haïront	ils haïraient

PRESENT SUBJUNCTIVE	PAST HISTORIC
je haïsse	**je haïs**
tu haïsses	**tu haïs**
il haïsse	**il haït**
nous haïssions	**nous haïmes**
vous haïssiez	**vous haïtes**
ils haïssent	**ils haïrent**

lire *to read*	Auxiliary: **avoir**

PAST PARTICIPLE	IMPERATIVE
lu	lis
	lisons
PRESENT PARTICIPLE	**lisez**
lisant	

PRESENT		IMPERFECT	
je	lis	je	lisais
tu	lis	tu	lisais
il	**lit**	**il**	**lisait**
nous	**lisons**	**nous**	**lisions**
vous	**lisez**	**vous**	**lisiez**
ils	**lisent**	**ils**	**lisaient**

FUTURE		CONDITIONAL	
je	lirai	je	lirais
tu	liras	tu	lirais
il	lira	il	lirait
nous	lirons	nous	lirions
vous	lirez	vous	liriez
ils	liront	ils	liraient

PRESENT SUBJUNCTIVE		PAST HISTORIC	
je	**lise**	**je**	**lus**
tu	**lises**	**tu**	**lus**
il	**lise**	**il**	**lut**
nous	**lisions**	**nous**	**lûmes**
vous	**lisiez**	**vous**	**lûtes**
ils	**lisent**	**ils**	**lurent**

mettre to put	Auxiliary: **avoir**

PAST PARTICIPLE	IMPERATIVE
mis	**mets**
	mettons
	mettez
PRESENT PARTICIPLE	
mettant	

PRESENT	IMPERFECT
je mets	je mettais
tu mets	tu mettais
il met	il mettait
nous mettons	nous mettions
vous mettez	vous mettiez
ils mettent	ils mettaient

FUTURE	CONDITIONAL
je mettrai	je mettrais
tu mettras	tu mettrais
il mettra	il mettrait
nous mettrons	nous mettrions
vous mettrez	vous mettriez
ils mettront	ils mettraient

PRESENT SUBJUNCTIVE	PAST HISTORIC
je mette	**je mis**
tu mettes	**tu mis**
il mette	**il mit**
nous mettions	**nous mîmes**
vous mettiez	**vous mîtes**
ils mettent	**ils mirent**

moudre _to grind_	Auxiliary: **avoir**

PAST PARTICIPLE	IMPERATIVE
moulu	mouds
	moulons
	moulez
PRESENT PARTICIPLE	
moulant	

PRESENT		IMPERFECT	
je	mouds	je	**moulais**
tu	mouds	tu	**moulais**
il	moud	il	**moulait**
nous	**moulons**	**nous**	**moulions**
vous	**moulez**	**vous**	**mouliez**
ils	**moulent**	**ils**	**moulaient**

FUTURE		CONDITIONAL	
je	moudrai	je	moudrais
tu	moudras	tu	moudrais
il	moudra	il	moudrait
nous	moudrons	nous	moudrions
vous	moudrez	vous	moudriez
ils	moudront	ils	moudraient

PRESENT SUBJUNCTIVE		PAST HISTORIC	
je	**moule**	**je**	**moulus**
tu	**moules**	**tu**	**moulus**
il	**moule**	**il**	**moulut**
nous	**moulions**	**nous**	**moulûmes**
vous	**mouliez**	**vous**	**moulûtes**
ils	**moulent**	**ils**	**moulurent**

mourir *to die*	Auxiliary: **être**

PAST PARTICIPLE

mort

PRESENT PARTICIPLE

mourant

IMPERATIVE

meurs
mourons
mourez

PRESENT	IMPERFECT
je **meurs**	je **mourais**
tu **meurs**	tu **mourais**
il **meurt**	il **mourait**
nous **mourons**	nous **mourions**
vous **mourez**	vous **mouriez**
ils **meurent**	ils **mouraient**

FUTURE	CONDITIONAL
je **mourrai**	je **mourrais**
tu **mourras**	tu **mourrais**
il **mourra**	il **mourrait**
nous **mourrons**	nous **mourrions**
vous **mourrez**	vous **mourriez**
ils **mourront**	ils **mourraient**

PRESENT SUBJUNCTIVE	PAST HISTORIC
je **meure**	je **mourus**
tu **meures**	tu **mourus**
il **meure**	il **mourut**
nous **mourions**	nous **mourûmes**
vous **mouriez**	vous **mourûtes**
ils **meurent**	ils **moururent**

naître *to be born*	Auxiliary: **être**

PAST PARTICIPLE   IMPERATIVE

né   nais
                                     naissons

PRESENT PARTICIPLE   naissez

naissant

PRESENT	IMPERFECT
je **nais**	je **naissais**
tu **nais**	tu **naissais**
il **naît**	il **naissait**
nous **naissons**	nous **naissions**
vous **naissez**	vous **naissiez**
ils **naissent**	ils **naissaient**

FUTURE	CONDITIONAL
je naîtrai	je naîtrais
tu naitras	tu naîtrais
il naîtra	il naîtrait
nous naîtrons	nous naîtrions
vous naîtrez	vous naîtriez
ils naîtront	ils naîtraient

PRESENT SUBJUNCTIVE	PAST HISTORIC
je **naisse**	je naquis
tu **naisses**	tu naquis
il **naisse**	il naquit
nous **naissions**	nous naquîmes
vous **naissiez**	vous naquîtes
ils **naissent**	ils naquirent

ouvrir *to open*	Auxiliary: **avoir**

PAST PARTICIPLE	IMPERATIVE
ouvert	**ouvre**
	ouvrons
	ouvrez
PRESENT PARTICIPLE	
ouvrant	

PRESENT		IMPERFECT	
	j'ouvre		**j'ouvrais**
tu	**ouvres**	tu	**ouvrais**
il	**ouvre**	il	**ouvrait**
nous	**ouvrons**	nous	**ouvrions**
vous	**ouvrez**	vous	**ouvriez**
ils	**ouvrent**	ils	**ouvraient**

FUTURE		CONDITIONAL	
	j'ouvrirai		j'ouvrirais
tu	ouvriras	tu	ouvrirais
il	ouvrira	il	ouvrirait
nous	ouvrirons	nous	ouvririons
vous	ouvrirez	vous	ouvririez
ils	ouvriront	ils	ouvriraient

PRESENT SUBJUNCTIVE		PAST HISTORIC	
	j'ouvre		j'ouvris
tu	**ouvres**	tu	ouvris
il	**ouvre**	il	ouvrit
nous	**ouvrions**	nous	ouvrîmes
vous	**ouvriez**	vous	ouvrîtes
ils	**ouvrent**	ils	ouvrirent

offrir *to offer*, **souffrir** *to suffer* are conjugated similarly

paraître to appear	Auxiliary: **avoir**

PAST PARTICIPLE

paru

PRESENT PARTICIPLE

paraissant

IMPERATIVE

parais
paraissons
paraissez

PRESENT	IMPERFECT
je **parais**	je **paraissais**
tu **parais**	tu **paraissais**
il **paraît**	il **paraissait**
nous **paraissons**	nous **paraissions**
vous **paraissez**	vous **paraissiez**
ils **paraissent**	ils **paraissaient**

FUTURE	CONDITIONAL
je paraîtrai	je paraîtrais
tu paraîtras	tu paraîtrais
il paraîtra	il paraîtrait
nous paraîtrons	nous paraîtrions
vous paraîtrez	vous paraîtriez
ils paraîtront	ils paraîtraient

PRESENT SUBJUNCTIVE	PAST HISTORIC
je **paraisse**	je **parus**
tu **paraisses**	tu **parus**
il **paraisse**	il **parut**
nous **paraissions**	nous **parûmes**
vous **paraissiez**	vous **parûtes**
ils **paraissent**	ils **parurent**

partir *to leave*	Auxiliary: **être**

PAST PARTICIPLE	IMPERATIVE
parti	**pars**
	partons
PRESENT PARTICIPLE	**partez**
partant	

PRESENT	IMPERFECT
je pars	**je partais**
tu pars	**tu partais**
il part	**il partait**
nous partons	**nous partions**
vous partez	**vous partiez**
ils partent	**ils partaient**

FUTURE	CONDITIONAL
je partirai	je partirais
tu partiras	tu partirais
il partira	il partirait
nous partirons	nous partirions
vous partirez	vous partiriez
ils partiront	ils partiraient

PRESENT SUBJUNCTIVE	PAST HISTORIC
je parte	je partis
tu partes	tu partis
il parte	il partit
nous partions	nous partîmes
vous partiez	vous partîtes
ils partent	ils partirent

plaire *to please*	Auxiliary: **avoir**
PAST PARTICIPLE	IMPERATIVE
plu	plais **plaisons** **plaisez**
PRESENT PARTICIPLE	
plaisant	

PRESENT	IMPERFECT
je plais	je plaisais
tu plais	tu plaisais
il **plaît**	il plaisait
nous plaisons	nous plaisions
vous plaisez	vous plaisiez
ils plaisent	ils plaisaient

FUTURE	CONDITIONAL
je plairai	je plairais
tu plairas	tu plairais
il plaira	il plairait
nous plairons	nous plairions
vous plairez	vous plairiez
ils plairont	ils plairaient

PRESENT SUBJUNCTIVE	PAST HISTORIC
je plaise	**je plus**
tu plaises	**tu plus**
il plaise	**il plut**
nous plaisions	**nous plûmes**
vous plaisiez	**vous plûtes**
ils plaisent	**ils plurent**

pleuvoir *to rain*	Auxiliary: **avoir**

PAST PARTICIPLE	IMPERATIVE
plu	*not used*

PRESENT PARTICIPLE

pleuvant

PRESENT	IMPERFECT
il **pleut**	il **pleuvait**

FUTURE	CONDITIONAL
il **pleuvra**	il **pleuvrait**

PRESENT SUBJUNCTIVE	PAST HISTORIC
il **pleuve**	il **plut**

pouvoir *to be able to*	Auxiliary: **avoir**
PAST PARTICIPLE	IMPERATIVE
pu	*not used*
PRESENT PARTICIPLE	
pouvant	

PRESENT	IMPERFECT
je **peux***	je **pouvais**
tu **peux**	tu **pouvais**
il **peut**	il **pouvait**
nous **pouvons**	nous **pouvions**
vous **pouvez**	vous **pouviez**
ils **peuvent**	ils **pouvaient**
FUTURE	**CONDITIONAL**
je **pourrai**	je **pourrais**
tu **pourras**	tu **pourrais**
il **pourra**	il **pourrait**
nous **pourrons**	nous **pourrions**
vous **pourrez**	vous **pourriez**
ils **pourront**	ils **pourraient**
PRESENT SUBJUNCTIVE	**PAST HISTORIC**
je **puisse**	je **pus**
tu **puisses**	tu **pus**
il **puisse**	il **put**
nous **puissions**	nous **pûmes**
vous **puissiez**	vous **pûtes**
ils **puissent**	ils **purent**

*In questions: **puis-je?**

prendre *to take*	Auxiliary: **avoir**

PAST PARTICIPLE	IMPERATIVE
pris	prends
	prenons
	prenez
PRESENT PARTICIPLE	
prenant	

PRESENT	IMPERFECT
je prends	je **prenais**
tu prends	tu **prenais**
il prend	il **prenait**
nous **prenons**	**nous** **prenions**
vous **prenez**	**nous** **preniez**
ils **prennent**	**ils** **prenaient**

FUTURE	CONDITIONAL
je prendrai	je prendrais
tu prendras	tu prendrais
il prendra	il prendrait
nous prendrons	nous prendrions
vous prendrez	vous prendriez
ils prendront	ils prendraient

PRESENT SUBJUNCTIVE	PAST HISTORIC
je **prenne**	je **pris**
tu **prennes**	tu **pris**
il **prenne**	il **prit**
nous **prenions**	**nous** **prîmes**
vous **preniez**	**vous** **prîtes**
ils **prennent**	**ils** **prirent**

recevoir to receive	Auxiliary: **avoir**

PAST PARTICIPLE	IMPERATIVE
reçu	reçois
	recevons
PRESENT PARTICIPLE	recevez
recevant	

PRESENT	IMPERFECT
je reçois	je recevais
tu reçois	tu recevais
il reçoit	il recevait
nous recevons	nous recevions
vous recevez	vous receviez
ils reçoivent	ils recevaient

FUTURE	CONDITIONAL
je recevrai	je recevrais
tu recevras	tu recevrais
il recevra	il recevrait
nous recevrons	nous recevrions
vous recevrez	vous recevriez
ils recevront	ils recevraient

PRESENT SUBJUNCTIVE	PAST HISTORIC
je reçoive	je reçus
tu reçoives	tu reçus
il reçoive	il reçut
nous recevions	nous reçûmes
vous receviez	vous reçûtes
ils reçoivent	ils reçurent

résoudre *to solve*	Auxiliary: **avoir**

PAST PARTICIPLE	IMPERATIVE
résolu	résous
	résolvons
	résolvez
PRESENT PARTICIPLE	
résolvant	

PRESENT		IMPERFECT	
je	résous	je	résolvais
tu	résous	tu	résolvais
il	résout	il	résolvait
nous	résolvons	nous	résolvions
vous	résolvez	vous	résolviez
ils	résolvent	ils	résolvaient

FUTURE		CONDITIONAL	
je	résoudrai	je	résoudrais
tu	résoudras	tu	résoudrais
il	résoudra	il	résoudrait
nous	résoudrons	nous	résoudrions
vous	résoudrez	vous	résoudriez
ils	résoudront	ils	résoudraient

PRESENT SUBJUNCTIVE		PAST HISTORIC	
je	résolve	je	résolus
tu	résolves	tu	résolus
il	résolve	il	résolut
nous	résolvions	nous	résolûmes
vous	résolviez	vous	résolûtes
ils	résolvent	ils	résolurent

rire *to laugh*	Auxiliary: **avoir**

PAST PARTICIPLE

ri

IMPERATIVE

ris
rions
riez

PRESENT PARTICIPLE

riant

PRESENT	IMPERFECT
je ris	je riais
tu ris	tu riais
il rit	il riait
nous rlons	nous riions
vous riez	vous riiez
ils rient	ils rlalent

FUTURE	CONDITIONAL
je rirai	je rirais
tu riras	tu rirais
il rira	il rirait
nous rirons	nous ririons
vous rirez	vous ririez
ils riront	ils riraient

PRESENT SUBJUNCTIVE	PAST HISTORIC
je rie	**je ris**
tu ries	**tu ris**
il rie	**il rit**
nous riions	**nous rîmes**
vous riiez	**vous rîtes**
ils rient	**ils rirent**

rompre *to break*   Auxiliary: **avoir**

PAST PARTICIPLE	IMPERATIVE
rompu	romps
	rompons
	rompez
PRESENT PARTICIPLE	
rompant	

PRESENT	IMPERFECT
je romps	je rompais
tu romps	tu rompais
il rompt	il rompait
nous rompons	nous rompions
vous rompez	vous rompiez
ils rompent	ils rompaient

FUTURE	CONDITIONAL
je romprai	je romprais
tu rompras	tu romprais
il rompra	il romprait
nous romprons	nous romprions
vous romprez	vous rompriez
ils rompront	ils rompraient

PRESENT SUBJUNCTIVE	PAST HISTORIC
je rompe	je rompis
tu rompes	tu rompis
il rompe	il rompit
nous rompions	nous rompîmes
vous rompiez	vous rompîtes
ils rompent	ils rompirent

savoir *to know*	Auxiliary: **avoir**

PAST PARTICIPLE	IMPERATIVE
su	
	sache
	sachons
	sachez
PRESENT PARTICIPLE	
sachant	

PRESENT	IMPERFECT
je sais	je savais
tu sais	tu savais
il sait	il savait
nous savons	nous savions
vous savez	vous saviez
ils savent	ils savaient

FUTURE	CONDITIONAL
je saurai	je saurais
tu sauras	tu saurais
il saura	il saurait
nous saurons	nous saurions
vous saurez	vous sauriez
ils sauront	ils sauraient

PRESENT SUBJUNCTIVE	PAST HISTORIC
je sache	je sus
tu saches	tu sus
il sache	il sut
nous sachions	nous sûmes
vous sachiez	vous sûtes
ils sachent	ils surent

sentir *to feel, to smell*	Auxiliary: **avoir**

PAST PARTICIPLE	IMPERATIVE
senti	**sens**
	sentons
	sentez
PRESENT PARTICIPLE	
sentant	

PRESENT	IMPERFECT
je **sens**	je **sentais**
tu **sens**	tu **sentais**
il **sent**	il **sentait**
nous **sentons**	nous **sentions**
vous **sentez**	vous **sentiez**
ils **sentent**	ils **sentaient**

FUTURE	CONDITIONAL
je sentirai	je sentirais
tu sentiras	tu sentirais
il sentira	il sentirait
nous sentirons	nous sentirions
vous sentirez	vous sentiriez
ils sentiront	ils sentiraient

PRESENT SUBJUNCTIVE	PAST HISTORIC
je **sente**	je sentis
tu **sentes**	tu sentis
il **sente**	il sentit
nous **sentions**	nous sentîmes
vous **sentiez**	vous sentîtes
ils **sentent**	ils sentirent

servir *to serve*	Auxiliary: **avoir**

PAST PARTICIPLE	IMPERATIVE
servi	**sers**
	servons
	servez
PRESENT PARTICIPLE	
servant	

PRESENT	IMPERFECT
je sers	**je servais**
tu sers	**tu servais**
il sert	**il servait**
nous servons	**nous servions**
vous servez	**vous serviez**
ils servent	**ils servaient**

FUTURE	CONDITIONAL
je servirai	je servirais
tu serviras	tu servirais
il servira	il servirait
nous servirons	nous servirions
vous servirez	vous serviriez
ils serviront	ils serviraient

PRESENT SUBJUNCTIVE	PAST HISTORIC
je serve	je servis
tu serves	tu servis
il serve	il servit
nous servions	nous servîmes
vous serviez	vous servîtes
ils servent	ils servirent

sortir *to go/come out*   Auxiliary: **être**

PAST PARTICIPLE   IMPERATIVE

sorti   **sors**
                                                          sortons
                                                          sortez
PRESENT PARTICIPLE

sortant

PRESENT	IMPERFECT
je sors	**je sortais**
tu sors	**tu sortais**
il sort	**il sortait**
nous sortons	**nous sortions**
vous sortez	**vous sortiez**
ils sortent	**ils sortaient**

FUTURE	CONDITIONAL
je sortirai	je sortirais
tu sortiras	tu sortirais
il sortira	il sortirait
nous sortirons	nous sortirions
vous sortirez	vous sortiriez
ils sortiront	ils sortiraient

PRESENT SUBJUNCTIVE	PAST HISTORIC
je sorte	je sortis
tu sortes	tu sortis
il sorte	il sortit
nous sortions	nous sortîmes
vous sortiez	vous sortîtes
ils sortent	ils sortirent

suffire *to be enough*	Auxiliary: **avoir**

PAST PARTICIPLE	IMPERATIVE
suffi	suffis
	suffisons
	suffisez
PRESENT PARTICIPLE	
suffisant	

PRESENT	IMPERFECT
je suffis	je **suffisais**
tu suffis	tu **suffisais**
il suffit	il **suffisait**
nous suffisons	**nous suffisions**
vous suffisez	**vous suffisiez**
ils suffisent	**ils suffisaient**

FUTURE	CONDITIONAL
je suffirai	je suffirais
tu suffiras	tu suffirais
il suffira	il suffirait
nous suffirons	nous suffirions
vous suffirez	vous suffiriez
ils suffiront	ils suffiraient

PRESENT SUBJUNCTIVE	PAST HISTORIC
je suffise	je **suffis**
tu suffises	tu **suffis**
il suffise	il **suffit**
nous suffisions	**nous suffîmes**
vous suffisiez	**vous suffîtes**
ils suffisent	**ils suffirent**

suivre to follow	Auxiliary: **avoir**

PAST PARTICIPLE

suivi

PRESENT PARTICIPLE

suivant

IMPERATIVE

suis
suivons
suivez

PRESENT	IMPERFECT
je **suis**	je suivais
tu **suis**	tu suivais
il **suit**	il suivait
nous suivons	nous suivions
vous suivez	vous suiviez
ils suivent	ils suivaient

FUTURE	CONDITIONAL
je suivrai	je suivrais
tu suivras	tu suivrais
il suivra	il suivrait
nous suivrons	nous suivrions
vous suivrez	vous suivriez
ils suivront	ils suivraient

PRESENT SUBJUNCTIVE	PAST HISTORIC
je suive	je suivis
tu suives	tu suivis
il suive	il suivit
nous suivions	nous suivîmes
vous suiviez	vous suivîtes
ils suivent	ils suivirent

se taire *to stop talking*	Auxiliary: **être**

PAST PARTICIPLE	IMPERATIVE
tu	tais-toi
	taisons-nous
PRESENT PARTICIPLE	**taisez-vous**
se taisant	

PRESENT		IMPERFECT	
je	me tais	je	**me taisais**
tu	te tais	tu	**te taisais**
il	se tait	il	**se taisait**
nous	**nous taisons**	**nous**	**nous taisions**
vous	**vous taisez**	**vous**	**vous taisiez**
ils	**se taisent**	**ils**	**se taisaient**

FUTURE		CONDITIONAL	
je	me tairai	je	me tairais
tu	te tairas	tu	te tairais
il	se taira	il	se tairait
nous	nous tairons	nous	nous tairions
vous	vous tairez	vous	vous tairiez
ils	se tairont	ils	se tairaient

PRESENT SUBJUNCTIVE		PAST HISTORIC	
je	**me taise**	**je**	**me tus**
tu	**te taises**	**tu**	**te tus**
il	**se taise**	**il**	**se tut**
nous	**nous taisions**	**nous**	**nous tûmes**
vous	**vous taisiez**	**vous**	**vous tûtes**
ils	**se taisent**	**ils**	**se turent**

tenir to hold	Auxiliary: **avoir**

PAST PARTICIPLE	IMPERATIVE
tenu	tiens
	tenons
	tenez
PRESENT PARTICIPLE	
tenant	

PRESENT		IMPERFECT	
je	tiens	je	tenais
tu	tiens	tu	tenais
il	tient	il	tenait
nous	tenons	nous	tenions
vous	tenez	vous	teniez
ils	tiennent	ils	tenaient

FUTURE		CONDITIONAL	
je	tiendrai	je	tiendrais
tu	tiendras	tu	tiendrais
il	tiendra	il	tiendrait
nous	tiendrons	nous	tiendrions
vous	tiendrez	vous	tiendriez
ils	tiendront	ils	tiendraient

PRESENT SUBJUNCTIVE		PAST HISTORIC	
je	tienne	je	tins
tu	tiennes	tu	tins
il	tienne	il	tint
nous	tenions	nous	tînmes
vous	teniez	vous	tîntes
ils	tiennent	ils	tinrent

| **vaincre** to defeat | Auxiliary: **avoir** |

PAST PARTICIPLE	IMPERATIVE
vaincu	vaincs
	vainquons
	vainquez
PRESENT PARTICIPLE	
vainquant	

PRESENT	IMPERFECT
je vaincs	je **vainquais**
tu vaincs	tu **vainquais**
il vainc	il **vainquait**
nous vainquons	**nous vainquions**
vous vainquez	**vous vainquiez**
ils vainquent	**ils vainquaient**

FUTURE	CONDITIONAL
je vaincrai	je vaincrais
tu vaincras	tu vaincrais
il vaincra	il vaincrait
nous vaincrons	nous vaincrions
vous vaincrez	vous vaincriez
ils vaincront	ils vaincraient

PRESENT SUBJUNCTIVE	PAST HISTORIC
je **vainque**	je **vainquis**
tu **vainques**	tu **vainquis**
il **vainque**	il **vainquit**
nous vainquions	**nous vainquîmes**
vous vainquiez	**vous vainquîtes**
ils vainquent	**ils vainquirent**

valoir *to be worth*	Auxiliary: **avoir**

PAST PARTICIPLE	IMPERATIVE
valu	vaux
	valons
	valez
PRESENT PARTICIPLE	
valant	

PRESENT		IMPERFECT	
je	vaux	je	valais
tu	vaux	tu	valais
il	vaut	il	valait
nous	valons	nous	valions
vous	valez	vous	valiez
ils	valent	ils	valaient

FUTURE		CONDITIONAL	
je	vaudrai	je	vaudrais
tu	vaudras	tu	vaudrais
il	vaudra	il	vaudrait
nous	vaudrons	nous	vaudrions
vous	vaudrez	vous	vaudriez
ils	vaudront	ils	vaudraient

PRESENT SUBJUNCTIVE		PAST HISTORIC	
je	vaille	je	valus
tu	vailles	tu	valus
il	vaille	il	valut
nous	valions	nous	valûmes
vous	valiez	vous	valûtes
ils	vaillent	ils	valurent

venir *to come*	Auxiliary: **être**

PAST PARTICIPLE	IMPERATIVE
venu	**viens**
	venons
	venez
PRESENT PARTICIPLE	
venant	

PRESENT	IMPERFECT
je **viens**	je **venais**
tu **viens**	tu **venais**
il **vient**	il **venait**
nous **venons**	nous **venions**
vous **venez**	vous **veniez**
ils **viennent**	ils **venaient**

FUTURE	CONDITIONAL
je **viendrai**	je **viendrais**
tu **viendras**	tu **viendrais**
il **viendra**	il **viendrait**
nous **viendrons**	nous **viendrions**
vous **viendrez**	vous **viendriez**
ils **viendront**	ils **viendraient**

PRESENT SUBJUNCTIVE	PAST HISTORIC
je **vienne**	je **vins**
tu **viennes**	tu **vins**
il **vienne**	il **vint**
nous **venions**	nous **vînmes**
vous **veniez**	vous **vîntes**
ils **viennent**	ils **vinrent**

vêtir to dress	Auxiliary: **avoir**

PAST PARTICIPLE	IMPERATIVE
vêtu	**vêts**
	vêtons
	vêtez
PRESENT PARTICIPLE	
vêtant	

PRESENT		IMPERFECT	
je	**vêts**	**je**	**vêtais**
tu	**vêts**	**tu**	**vêtais**
il	**vêt**	**il**	**vêtait**
nous	**vêtons**	**nous**	**vêtions**
vous	**vêtez**	**vous**	**vêtiez**
ils	**vêtent**	**ils**	**vêtaient**

FUTURE		CONDITIONAL	
je	vêtirai	je	vêtirais
tu	vêtiras	tu	vêtirais
il	vêtira	il	vêtirait
nous	vêtirons	nous	vêtirions
vous	vêtirez	vous	vêtiriez
ils	vêtiront	ils	vêtiraient

PRESENT SUBJUNCTIVE		PAST HISTORIC	
je	**vête**	je	vêtis
tu	**vêtes**	tu	vêtis
il	**vête**	il	vêtit
nous	**vêtions**	nous	vêtîmes
vous	**vêtiez**	vous	vêtîtes
ils	**vêtent**	ils	vêtirent

vivre *to live*	Auxiliary: **avoir**

PAST PARTICIPLE	IMPERATIVE
vécu	**vis**
	vivons
	vivez
PRESENT PARTICIPLE	
vivant	

PRESENT		IMPERFECT	
je	**vis**	je	vivais
tu	**vis**	tu	vivais
il	**vit**	il	vivait
nous	vivons	nous	vivions
vous	vivez	vous	viviez
ils	vivent	ils	vivaient

FUTURE		CONDITIONAL	
je	vivrai	je	vivrais
tu	vivras	tu	vivrais
il	vivra	il	vivrait
nous	vivrons	nous	vivrions
vous	vivrez	vous	vivriez
ils	vivront	ils	vivraient

PRESENT SUBJUNCTIVE		PAST HISTORIC	
je	vive	**je**	**vécus**
tu	vives	**tu**	**vécus**
il	vive	**il**	**vécut**
nous	vivions	**nous**	**vécûmes**
vous	viviez	**vous**	**vécûtes**
ils	vivent	**ils**	**vécurent**

voir to see	Auxiliary: **avoir**
PAST PARTICIPLE	IMPERATIVE
vu	vois voyons voyez
PRESENT PARTICIPLE	
voyant	

PRESENT	IMPERFECT
je vois	je voyais
tu vois	tu voyais
il voit	il voyait
nous voyons	nous voyions
vous voyez	vous voyiez
ils voient	ils voyaient

FUTURE	CONDITIONAL
je verrai	je verrais
tu verras	tu verrais
il verra	il verrait
nous verrons	nous verrions
vous verrez	vous verriez
ils verront	ils verraient

PRESENT SUBJUNCTIVE	PAST HISTORIC
je voie	je vis
tu voies	tu vis
il voie	il vit
nous voyions	nous vîmes
vous voyiez	vous vîtes
ils voient	ils virent

vouloir *to wish, want*	Auxiliary: **avoir**

PAST PARTICIPLE

voulu

IMPERATIVE

veuille
veuillons
veuillez

PRESENT PARTICIPLE

voulant

PRESENT	IMPERFECT
je **veux**	je **voulais**
tu **veux**	tu **voulais**
il **veut**	il **voulait**
nous **voulons**	nous **voulions**
vous **voulez**	vous **vouliez**
ils **veulent**	ils **voulaient**

FUTURE	CONDITIONAL
je **voudrai**	je **voudrais**
tu **voudras**	tu **voudrais**
il **voudra**	il **voudrait**
nous **voudrons**	nous **voudrions**
vous **voudrez**	vous **voudriez**
ils **voudront**	ils **voudraient**

PRESENT SUBJUNCTIVE	PAST HISTORIC
je **veuille**	je **voulus**
tu **veuilles**	tu **voulus**
il **veuille**	il **voulut**
nous **voulions**	nous **voulûmes**
vous **vouliez**	vous **voulûtes**
ils **veuillent**	ils **voulurent**

❐ The Gender of Nouns

In French, all nouns are either masculine or feminine, whether denoting people, animals or things. Unlike English, there is no neuter gender for inanimate objects and abstract nouns.

Gender is largely unpredictable and has to be learnt for each noun. However, the following guidelines will help you determine the gender for certain types of nouns.

◆ Nouns denoting male people and animals are usually – but not always – masculine, e.g.

un homme	**un taureau**
a man	*a bull*
un infirmier	**un cheval**
a (male) nurse	*a horse*

◆ Nouns denoting female people and animals are usually – but not always – feminine, e.g.

une fille	**une vache**
a girl	*a cow*
une infirmière	**une brebis**
a nurse	*a ewe*

◆ Some nouns are masculine OR feminine depending on the sex of the person to whom they refer, e.g.

un camarade	**une camarade**
a (male) friend	*a (female) friend*
un Belge	**une Belge**
a Belgian (man)	*a Belgian (woman)*

◆ Other nouns referring to either men or women have only one gender which applies to both, e.g.

un professeur	**une personne**	**une sentinelle**
a teacher	*a person*	*a sentry*
un témoin	**une victime**	**une recrue**
a witness	*a victim*	*a recruit*

- Sometimes the ending of the noun indicates its gender. Shown below are some of the most important to guide you:

Masculine endings

-age	**le courage** *courage*, **le rinçage** *rinsing*
	EXCEPTIONS: **une cage** *a cage*, **une image** *a picture*, **la nage** *swimming*, **une page** *a page*, **une plage** *a beach*, **une rage** *a rage*
-ment	**le commencement** *the beginning*
	EXCEPTION: **une jument** *a mare*
-oir	**un couloir** *a corridor*, **un miroir** *a mirror*
-sme	**le pessimisme** *pessimism*, **l'enthousiasme** *enthusiasm*

Feminine endings

-ance, anse	**la confiance** *confidence*, **la danse** *dancing*
-ence, -ense	**la prudence** *caution*, **la défense** *defence*
	EXCEPTION: **le silence** *silence*
-ion	**une région** *a region*, **une addition** *a bill*
	EXCEPTIONS: **un pion** *a pawn*, **un espion** *a spy*
-oire	**une baignoire** *a bath(tub)*
-té, -tié	**la beauté** *beauty*, **la moitié** *half*

- Suffixes which differentiate between male and female are shown on pp 134 and 136.

- The following words have different meanings depending on gender:

le crêpe	*crêpe*	**la crêpe**	*pancake*
le livre	*book*	**la livre**	*pound*
le manche	*handle*	**la manche**	*sleeve*
le mode	*method*	**la mode**	*fashion*
le moule	*mould*	**la moule**	*mussel*
le page	*page(boy)*	**la page**	*page (in book)*
le physique	*physique*	**la physique**	*physics*
le poêle	*stove*	**la poêle**	*frying pan*
le somme	*nap*	**la somme**	*sum*
le tour	*turn*	**la tour**	*tower*
le voile	*veil*	**la voile**	*sail*

Grammar

❑ Gender: the Formation of Feminines

As in English, male and female are sometimes differentiated by the use of two quite separate words, e.g.

mon oncle	**ma tante**
my uncle	*my aunt*
un taureau	**une vache**
a bull	*a cow*

There are, however, some words in French which show this distinction by the form of their ending.

◆ Some nouns add an **e** to the masculine singular form to form the feminine → 1

◆ If the masculine singular form already ends in **-e**, no further **e** is added in the feminine → 2

◆ Some nouns undergo a further change when **e** is added. These changes occur regularly and are shown on p 136.

Feminine forms to note

MASCULINE	FEMININE	
un âne	une ânesse	donkey
le comte	la comtesse	count/countess
le duc	la duchesse	duke/duchess
un Esquimau	une Esquimaude	Eskimo
le fou	la folle	madman/madwoman
le Grec	la Grecque	Greek
un hôte	une hôtesse	host/hostess
le jumeau	la jumelle	twin
le maître	la maîtresse	master/mistress
le prince	la princesse	prince/princess
le tigre	la tigresse	tiger/tigress
le traître	la traîtresse	traitor
le Turc	la Turque	Turk
le vieux	la vieille	old man/old woman

1   **un ami**   **une amie**
      a (male) friend   a (female) friend
      un employé   **une employée**
      a (male) employee   a (female) employee
      un Français   **une Française**
      a Frenchman   a Frenchwoman

2   **un élève**   **une élève**
      a (male) pupil   a (female) pupil
      un collègue   **une collègue**
      a (male) colleague   a (female) colleague
      un camarade   **une camarade**
      a (male) friend   a (female) friend

☐ Regular feminine endings

MASC. SING.	FEM. SING.	
-f	-ve	→ 1
-x	-se	→ 2
-eur	-euse	→ 3
-teur	{ -teuse	→ 4
	-trice	→ 5

Some nouns double the final consonant before adding **e**:

MASC. SING.	FEM. SING.	
-an	-anne	→ 6
-en	-enne	→ 7
-on	-onne	→ 8
-et	-ette	→ 9
-el	-elle	→ 10

Some nouns add an accent to the final syllable before adding **e**:

MASC. SING.	FEM. SING.	
-er	-ère	→ 11

Pronunciation and feminine endings

This is dealt with on p 244.

Grammar

1	**un sportif** a sportsman **un veuf** a widower	**une sportive** a sportswoman **une veuve** a widow
2	**un époux** a husband **un amoureux** a man in love	**une épouse** a wife **une amoureuse** a woman in love
3	**un danseur** a dancer **un voleur** a thief	**une danseuse** a dancer **une voleuse** a thief
4	**un menteur** a liar **un chanteur** a singer	**une menteuse** a liar **une chanteuse** a singer
5	**un acteur** an actor **un conducteur** a driver	**une actrice** an actress **une conductrice** a driver
6	**un paysan** a countryman	**une paysanne** a countrywoman
7	**un Parisien** a Parisian	**une Parisienne** a Parisian (woman)
8	**un baron** a baron	**une baronne** a baroness
9	**le cadet** the youngest (child)	**la cadette** the youngest (child)
10	**un intellectuel** an intellectual	**une intellectuelle** an intellectual
11	**un étranger** a foreigner **le dernier** the last (one)	**une étrangère** a foreigner **la dernière** the last (one)

❏ The Formation of Plurals

◆ Most nouns add **s** to the singular form → ①

◆ When the singular form already ends in **-s**, **-x** or **-z**, no further **s** is added → ②

◆ For nouns ending in **-au**, **-eau** or **-eu**, the plural ends in **-aux**, **-eaux** or **-eux** → ③

EXCEPTIONS:

pneu	*tyre*	(plur: **pneus**)
bleu	*bruise*	(plur: **bleus**)

◆ For nouns ending in **-al** or **-ail**, the plural ends in **-aux** → ④

EXCEPTIONS:

bal	*ball*	(plur: **bals**)
festival	*festival*	(plur: **festivals**)
chandail	*sweater*	(plur: **chandails**)
détail	*detail*	(plur: **détails**)

◆ Forming the plural of compound nouns is complicated and you are advised to check each one individually in a dictionary.

Irregular plural forms

◆ Some masculine nouns ending in **-ou** add **x** in the plural. These are:

bijou	*jewel*	**genou**	*knee*	**joujou**	*toy*
caillou	*pebble*	**hibou**	*owl*	**pou**	*louse*
chou	*cabbage*				

◆ Some other nouns are totally unpredictable. Chief among these are:

SINGULAR		PLURAL
œil	*eye*	**yeux**
ciel	*sky*	**cieux**
Monsieur	*Mr*	**Messieurs**
Madame	*Mrs*	**Mesdames**
Mademoiselle	*Miss*	**Mesdemoiselles**

Pronunciation of plural forms

This is dealt with on p 244.

1. **le jardin**   **les jardins**
   the garden   the gardens
   une voiture   **des voitures**
   a car   (some) cars
   l'hôtel   **les hôtels**
   the hotel   the hotels

2. **un tas**   **des tas**
   a heap   (some) heaps
   une voix   **des voix**
   a voice   (some) voices
   le gaz   **les gaz**
   the gas   the gases

3. **un tuyau**   **des tuyaux**
   a pipe   (some) pipes
   le chapeau   **les chapeaux**
   the hat   the hats
   le feu   **les feux**
   the fire   the fires

4. **le journal**   **les journaux**
   the newspaper   the newspapers
   un travail   **des travaux**
   a job   (some) jobs

◻ The Definite Article

	WITH MASC. NOUN	WITH FEM. NOUN	
SING.	le (l')	la (l')	*the*
PLUR.	les	les	*the*

- The gender and number of the noun determines the form of the article → [1]

- **le** and **la** change to **l'** before a vowel or an **h** 'mute' → [2]

- For uses of the definite article see p 142.

- **à + le/la (l'), à + les**

	WITH MASC. NOUN	WITH FEM. NOUN	
SING.	au (à l')	à la (à l')	
PLUR.	aux	aux	→ [3]

- The definite article combines with the preposition **à**, as shown above. You should pay particular attention to the masculine singular form **au,** and both plural forms **aux,** since these are not visually the sum of their parts.

- **de + le/la (l'), de + les**

	WITH MASC. NOUN	WITH FEM. NOUN	
SING.	du (de l')	de la (de l')	
PLUR.	des	des	→ [4]

- The definite article combines with the preposition **de**, as shown above. You should pay particular attention to the masculine singular form **du,** and both plural forms **des,** since these are not visually the sum of their parts.

Grammar

MASCULINE	FEMININE
1 **le train**	**la gare**
the train	the station
le garçon	**la fille**
the boy	the girl
les hôtels	**les écoles**
the hotels	the schools
les professeurs	**les femmes**
the teachers	the women
2 **l'acteur**	**l'actrice**
the actor	the actress
l'effet	**l'eau**
the effect	the water
l'ingrédient	**l'idée**
the ingredient	the idea
l'objet	**l'ombre**
the object	the shadow
l'univers	**l'usine**
the universe	the factory
l'hôpital	**l'heure**
the hospital	the time
3 **au cinéma**	**à la bibliothèque**
at/to the cinema	at/to the library
à l'employé	**à l'infirmière**
to the employee	to the nurse
à l'hôpital	**à l'hôtesse**
at/to the hospital	to the hostess
aux étudiants	**aux maisons**
to the students	to the houses
4 **du bureau**	**de la réunion**
from/of the office	from/of the meeting
de l'auteur	**de l'Italienne**
from/of the author	from/of the Italian woman
de l'hôte	**de l'horloge**
from/of the host	of the clock
des États-Unis	**des vendeuses**
from/of the United States	from/of the saleswomen

❏ Uses of the Definite Article

While the definite article is used in much the same way in French as it is in English, its use is more widespread in French. Unlike English the definite article is also used:

- with abstract nouns, except when following certain prepositions → 1

- in generalizations, especially with plural or uncountable* nouns → 2

- with names of countries → 3
  EXCEPTIONS: no article with countries following **en** *to/in* → 4

- with parts of the body → 5
  'Ownership' is often indicated by an indirect object pronoun or a reflexive pronoun → 6

- in expressions of quantity/rate/price → 7

- with titles/ranks/professions followed by a proper name → 8

- The definite article is NOT used with nouns in apposition → 9

*An uncountable noun is one which cannot be used in the plural or with an indefinite article, e.g. **l'acier** *steel,* **le lait** *milk.*

Grammar

1. **Les prix montent**
Prices are rising
L'amour rayonne dans ses yeux
Love shines in his eyes
BUT   **avec plaisir**   **sans espoir**
      with pleasure   without hope

2. **Je n'aime pas le café**
I don't like coffee
Les enfants ont besoin d'être aimés
Children need to be loved

3. **le Japon**   **la France**   **l'Italie**   **les Pays-Bas**
   Japan   France   Italy   The Netherlands

4. **aller en Écosse**   **Il travaille en Allemagne**
   to go to Scotland   He works in Germany

5. **Tournez la tête à gauche**
Turn your head to the left
j'ai mal à la gorge
My throat is sore, I have a sore throat

6. **La tête me tourne**
My head is spinning
Elle s'est brossé les dents
She brushed her teeth

7. **40 francs le mètre/le kilo/la douzaine/la pièce**
40 francs a metre/a kilo/a dozen/each
rouler à 80 km à l'heure
to go at 50 m.p.h.
payé à l'heure/au jour/au mois
paid by the hour/by the day/by the month

8. **le roi Georges III**   **le capitaine Darbeau**
   King George III   Captain Darbeau
le docteur Rousseau   **Monsieur le président**
   Dr Rousseau   Mr Chairman/President

9. **Victor Hugo, grand écrivain du dix-neuvième siècle**
Victor Hugo, a great author of the nineteenth century
Joseph Leblanc, inventeur et entrepreneur, a été le premier ...
Joseph Leblanc, an inventor and entrepreneur, was the first ...

□ The Partitive Article

The partitive article has the sense of *some* or *any*, although the French is not always translated in English.

Forms of the partitive

	WITH MASC. NOUN	WITH FEM. NOUN	
SING.	**du (de l')**	**de la (de l')**	*some, any*
PLUR.	**des**	**des**	*some, any*

- The gender and number of the noun determines the form of the partitive → ①

- The forms shown in brackets are used before a vowel or an **h** 'mute' → ②

- **des** becomes **de** (**d'** + vowel) before an adjective → ③, unless the adjective and noun are seen as forming one unit → ④

- In negative sentences **de** (**d'** + vowel) is used for both genders, singular and plural → ⑤

  EXCEPTION: after **ne ... que** *only*, the positive forms above are used → ⑥

1. **Avez-vous du sucre?**
   Have you any sugar?
   J'ai acheté de la farine et de la margarine
   I bought (some) flour and margarine
   Il a mangé des gâteaux
   He ate some cakes
   Est-ce qu'il y a des lettres pour moi?
   Are there (any) letters for me?

2. **Il me doit de l'argent**
   He owes me (some) money
   C'est de l'histoire ancienne
   That's ancient history

3. **Il a fait de gros efforts pour nous aider**
   He made a great effort to help us
   Cette région a de belles églises
   This region has some beautiful churches

4. **des grandes vacances**   **des jeunes gens**
   summer holidays   young people

5. **Je n'ai pas de nourriture/d'argent**
   I don't have any food/money
   Vous n'avez pas de timbres/d'œufs?
   Have you no stamps/eggs?
   Je ne mange jamais de viande/d'omelettes
   I never eat meat/omelettes
   Il ne veut plus de visiteurs/d'eau
   He doesn't want any more visitors/water

6. **Il ne boit que du thé/de la bière/de l'eau**
   He only drinks tea/beer/water
   Je n'ai que des problèmes avec cette machine
   I have nothing but problems with this machine

▢ The Indefinite Article

	WITH MASC. NOUN	WITH FEM. NOUN	
SING.	**un**	**une**	*a*
PLUR.	**des**	**des**	*some*

* **des** is also the plural of the partitive article (see p 144).

* In negative sentences, **de** (**d'** + vowel) is used for both singular and plural → ①

* The indefinite article is used in French largely as it is in English EXCEPT:

  – there is no article when a person's profession is being stated → ②
    The article *is* present however, following **ce** (**c'** + vowel) → ③

  – the English article is not translated by **un/une** in constructions like *what a surprise, what an idiot* → ④

  – in structures of the type given in example ⑤ the article **un/une** is used in French and not translated in English → ⑤

1. **Je n'ai pas de livre/d'enfants**
   I don't have a book/(any) children

2. **Il est professeur**   **Ma mère est infirmière**
   He's a teacher   My mother's a nurse

3. **C'est un médecin**   **Ce sont des acteurs**
   He's/She's a doctor   They're actors

4. **Quelle surprise!**   **Quel dommage!**
   What a surprise!   What a shame!

5. **avec une grande sagesse/un courage admirable**
   with great wisdom /admirable courage
   Il a fait preuve d'un sang-froid incroyable
   He showed incredible coolness
   Un produit d'une qualité incomparable
   A product of incomparable quality

◻ Adjectives

Most adjectives agree in number and in gender with the noun or pronoun.

The formation of feminines

- Most adjectives add an **e** to the masculine singular form → ①

- If the masculine singular form already ends in **-e**, no further **e** is added → ②

- Some adjectives undergo a further change when **e** is added. These changes occur regularly and are shown on p 150.

- Irregular feminine forms are shown on p 152.

The formation of plurals

- The plural of both regular and irregular adjectives is formed by adding an **s** to the masculine or feminine singular form, as appropriate → ③

- When the masculine singular form already ends in **-s** or **-x**, no further **s** is added → ④

- For masculine singulars ending in **-au** and **-eau**, the masculine plural is **-aux** and **-eaux** → ⑤

- For masculine singulars ending in **-al**, the masculine plural is **-aux** → ⑥

EXCEPTIONS:	**final**	(masculine plural **finals**)
	fatal	(masculine plural **fatals**)
	naval	(masculine plural **navals**)

Pronunciation of feminine and plural adjectives

This is dealt with on p 244.

1 **mon frère aîné**
my elder brother
le petit garçon
the little boy
un sac gris
a grey bag
un bruit fort
a loud noise

ma sœur aînée
my elder sister
la petite fille
the little girl
une chemise grise
a grey shirt
une voix forte
a loud voice

2 **un jeune homme**
a young man
l'autre verre
the other glass

une jeune femme
a young woman
l'autre assiette
the other plate

3 **le dernier train**
the last train
une vieille maison
an old house
un long voyage
a long journey
la rue étroite
the narrow street

les derniers trains
the last trains
de vieilles maisons
old houses
de longs voyages
long journeys
les rues étroites
the narrow streets

4 **un diplomate français**
a French diplomat
un homme dangereux
a dangerous man

des diplomates français
French diplomats
des hommes dangereux
dangerous men

5 **le nouveau professeur**
the new teacher
un chien esquimau
a husky (Fr. = an Eskimo dog)

les nouveaux professeurs
the new teachers
des chiens esquimaux
huskies (Fr. = Eskimo dogs)

6 **un ami loyal**
a loyal friend
un geste amical
a friendly gesture

des amis loyaux
loyal friends
des gestes amicaux
friendly gestures

◻ Regular feminine endings

MASC. SING.	FEM. SING.	EXAMPLES	
-f	-ve	neuf, vif	→ 1
-x	-se	heureux, jaloux	→ 2
-eur	-euse	travailleur, flâneur	→ 3
-teur	{ -teuse	flatteur, menteur	→ 4
	{ -trice	destructeur, séducteur	→ 5

EXCEPTIONS:

bref: see p 152

doux, faux, roux, vieux: see p 152

extérieur, inférieur, intérieur, meilleur, supérieur: all add **e** to the masculine

enchanteur: fem. = **enchanteresse**

MASC. SING.	FEM. SING.	EXAMPLES	
-an	-anne	paysan	→ 6
-en	-enne	ancien, parisien	→ 7
-on	-onne	bon, breton	→ 8
-as	-asse	bas, las	→ 9
-et*	-ette	muet, violet	→ 10
-el	-elle	annuel, mortel	→ 11
-eil	-eille	pareil, vermeil	→ 12

EXCEPTION:

ras: fem. = **rase**

MASC. SING.	FEM. SING.	EXAMPLES	
-et*	-ète	secret, complet	→ 13
-er	-ère	étranger, fier	→ 14

*Note that there are two feminine endings for masculine adjectives ending in **-et**.

1	**un résultat positif** a positive result	**une attitude positive** a positive attitude
2	**d'un ton sérieux** in a serious tone (of voice)	**une voix sérieuse** a serious voice
3	**un enfant trompeur** a deceitful child	**une déclaration trompeuse** a misleading statement
4	**un tableau flatteur** a flattering picture	**une comparaison flatteuse** a flattering comparison
5	**un geste protecteur** a protective gesture	**une couche protectrice** a protective layer
6	**un problème paysan** a farming problem	**la vie paysanne** country life
7	**un avion égyptien** an Egyptian plane	**une statue égyptienne** an Egyptian statue
8	**un bon repas** a good meal	**de bonne humeur** in a good mood
9	**un plafond bas** a low ceiling	**à voix basse** in a low voice
10	**un travail net** a clean piece of work	**une explication nette** a clear explanation
11	**un homme cruel** a cruel man	**une remarque cruelle** a cruel remark
12	**un livre pareil** such a book	**en pareille occasion** on such an occasion
13	**un regard inquiet** an anxious look	**une attente inquiète** an anxious wait
14	**un goût amer** a bitter taste	**une amère déception** a bitter disappointment

☐ Adjectives with irregular feminine forms

MASC. SING.	FEM. SING.		
aigu	aiguë	*sharp; high-pitched*	→ 1
ambigu	ambiguë	*ambiguous*	
beau (bel)*	belle	*beautiful*	
bénin	bénigne	*benign*	
blanc	blanche	*white*	
bref	brève	*brief, short*	→ 2
doux	douce	*soft; sweet*	
épais	épaisse	*thick*	
esquimau	esquimaude	*Eskimo*	
faux	fausse	*wrong*	
favori	favorite	*favourite*	→ 3
fou (fol)*	folle	*mad*	
frais	fraîche	*fresh*	→ 4
franc	franche	*frank*	
gentil	gentille	*kind*	
grec	grecque	*Greek*	
gros	grosse	*big*	
jumeau	jumelle	*twin*	→ 5
long	longue	*long*	
malin	maligne	*malignant*	
mou (mol)*	molle	*soft*	
nouveau (nouvel)*	nouvelle	*new*	
nul	nulle	*no*	
public	publique	*public*	→ 6
roux	rousse	*red-haired*	
sec	sèche	*dry*	
sot	sotte	*foolish*	
turc	turque	*Turkish*	
vieux (vieil)*	vieille	*old*	

*This form is used when the following word begins with a vowel or an **h** 'mute' → 7

1. **un son aigu**
a high-pitched sound

   une douleur aiguë
a sharp pain

2. **un bref discours**
a short speech

   une brève rencontre
a short meeting

3. **mon sport favori**
my favourite sport

   ma chanson favorite
my favourite song

4. **du pain frais**
fresh bread

   de la crème fraîche
fresh cream

5. **mon frère jumeau**
my twin brother

   ma sœur jumelle
my twin sister

6. **un jardin public**
a (public) park

   l'opinion publique
public opinion

7. **un bel appartement**
a beautiful flat
le nouvel inspecteur
the new inspector
un vieil arbre
an old tree

   un bel habit
a beautiful outfit
un nouvel harmonica
a new harmonica
un vieil hôtel
an old hotel

□ Comparatives and Superlatives

Comparatives

These are formed using the following constructions:

plus ... (que)	*more ... (than)*	→ 1
moins ... (que)	*less ... (than)*	→ 2
aussi ... que	*as ... as*	→ 3
si ... que*	*as ... as*	→ 4

*used mainly after a negative

Superlatives

These are formed using the following constructions:

le/la/les plus ... (que)	*the most ... (that)*	→ 5
le/la/les moins ... (que)	*the least ... (that)*	→ 6

- When the possessive adjective is present, two constructions are possible → 7
- After a superlative the preposition **de** is often translated as *in* → 8
- If a clause follows a superlative, the verb is in the subjunctive → 9

Adjectives with irregular comparatives/superlatives

ADJECTIVE	COMPARATIVE	SUPERLATIVE
bon *good*	**meilleur** *better*	**le meilleur** *the best*
mauvais *bad*	**pire** OR **plus mauvais** *worse*	**le pire** OR **le plus mauvais** *the worst*
petit *small*	**moindre*** OR **plus petit** *smaller; lesser*	**le moindre*** OR **le plus petit** *the smallest; the least*

*used only with abstract nouns

- Comparative and superlative adjectives agree in number and in gender with the noun, just like any other adjective → 10

1. **une raison plus grave**
   a more serious reason
   Elle est plus petite que moi
   She is smaller than me

2. **un film moins connu**
   a less well-known film
   C'est moins cher qu'il ne pense
   It's cheaper than he thinks

3. **Robert était aussi inquiet que moi**
   Robert was as worried as I was
   Cette ville n'est pas aussi grande que Bordeaux
   This town isn't as big as Bordeaux

4. **Ils ne sont pas si contents que ça**
   They aren't as happy as all that

5. **le guide le plus utile**   **la voiture la plus petite**
   the most useful guidebook   the smallest car
   les plus grandes maisons
   the biggest houses

6. **le mois le moins agréable**   **la fille la moins forte**
   the least pleasant month   the weakest girl
   les moins belles peintures
   the least attractive paintings

7. **Mon désir le plus cher** } **est de voyager**
   Mon plus cher désir
   My dearest wish is to travel

8. **la plus grande gare de Londres**
   the biggest station in London
   l'habitant le plus âgé du village/de la région
   the oldest inhabitant in the village/in the area

9. **la personne la plus gentille que je connaisse**
   the nicest person I know

10. **les moindres difficultés**
    the least difficulties
    la meilleure qualité
    the best quality

☐ Demonstrative Adjectives

	MASCULINE	FEMININE	
SING.	**ce (cet)**	**cette**	*this; that*
PLUR.	**ces**	**ces**	*these; those*

◆ Demonstrative adjectives agree in number and gender with the noun → ☐1

◆ **cet** is used when the following word begins with a vowel or an **h** 'mute' → ☐2

◆ For emphasis or in order to distinguish between people or objects, **-ci** or **-là** is added to the noun: **-ci** indicates proximity (usually translated *this*) and **là** distance *(that)* → ☐3

1. **Ce stylo ne marche pas**
   This/That pen isn't working
   Comment s'appelle cette entreprise?
   What's this/that company called?
   Ces livres sont les miens
   These/Those books are mine
   Ces couleurs sont plus jolies
   These/Those colours are nicer

2. **cet oiseau**
   this/that bird
   cet article
   this/that article
   cet homme
   this/that man

3. **Comblen coûte ce manteau-cl?**
   How much is this coat?
   Je voudrais cinq de ces pommes-là
   I'd like five of those apples
   Est-ce que tu reconnais cette personne-là?
   Do you recognize that person?
   Mettez ces vêtements-cl dans cette vallse-là
   Put these clothes in that case
   Ce garçon-là appartient à ce groupe-ci
   That boy belongs to this group

☐ Interrogative Adjectives

	MASCULINE	FEMININE	
SING.	**quel?**	**quelle?**	*what?; which?*
PLUR.	**quels?**	**quelles?**	*what?; which?*

- Interrogative adjectives agree in number and gender with the noun
  → ①

- The forms shown above are also used in indirect questions → ②

☐ Exclamatory Adjectives

	MASCULINE	FEMININE	
SING.	**quel!**	**quelle!**	*what (a)!*
PLUR.	**quels!**	**quelles!**	*what!*

- Exclamatory adjectives agree in number and gender with the noun
  → ③

- For other exclamations, see p 214.

1. **Quel genre d'homme est-ce?**
   What type of man is he?
   Quelle est leur décision?
   What is their decision?
   Vous jouez de quels instruments?
   What instruments do you play?
   Quelles offres avez-vous reçues?
   What offers have you received?
   Quel vin recommandez-vous?
   Which wine do you recommend?
   Quelles couleurs préférez-vous?
   Which colours do you prefer?

2. **Je ne sais pas à quelle heure il est arrivé**
   I don't know what time he arrived
   Dites-moi quels sont les livres les plus intéressants
   Tell me which books are the most interesting

3. **Quel dommage!**
   What a pity!
   Quelle idée!
   What an idea!
   Quels beaux livres vous avez!
   What fine books you have!
   Quelles jolies fleurs!
   What nice flowers!

□ **Possessive Adjectives**

WITH SING. NOUN		WITH PLUR. NOUN	
MASC.	FEM.	MASC./FEM.	
mon	ma (mon)	mes	*my*
ton	ta (ton)	tes	*your*
son	sa (son)	ses	*his; her; its*
notre	notre	nos	*our*
votre	votre	vos	*your*
leur	leur	leurs	*their*

- Possessive adjectives agree in number and gender with the noun, NOT WITH THE OWNER → ①

- The forms shown in brackets are used when the following word begins with a vowel or an **h** 'mute' → ②

- **son, sa, ses** have the additional meaning of *one's* → ③

1. **Catherine a oublié son parapluie**
   Catherine has left her umbrella
   Paul cherche sa montre
   Paul's looking for his watch
   Mon frère et ma sœur habitent à Glasgow
   My brother and sister live in Glasgow
   Est-ce que tes voisins ont vendu leur voiture?
   Did your neighbours sell their car?
   Rangez vos affaires
   Put your things away

2. **mon appareil-photo**
   my camera
   ton histoire
   your story
   son erreur
   his/her mistake
   mon autre sœur
   my other sister

3. **perdre son équilibre**
   to lose one's balance
   présenter ses excuses
   to offer one's apologies

▢ Position of Adjectives

- French adjectives usually follow the noun → ①

- Adjectives of colour or nationality *always* follow the noun → ②

- As in English, demonstrative, possessive, numerical and interrogative adjectives precede the noun → ③

- The adjectives **autre** *other* and **chaque** *each, every* precede the noun → ④

- The following common adjectives can precede the noun:

beau	*beautiful*	**jeune**	*young*
bon	*good*	**joli**	*pretty*
court	*short*	**long**	*long*
dernier	*last*	**mauvais**	*bad*
grand	*great*	**petit**	*small*
gros	*big*	**tel**	*such (a)*
haut	*high*	**vieux**	*old*

- The meaning of the following adjectives varies according to their position:

	BEFORE NOUN	AFTER NOUN	
ancien	*former*	*old, ancient*	→ ⑤
brave	*good*	*brave*	→ ⑥
cher	*dear (beloved)*	*expensive*	→ ⑦
grand	*great*	*tall*	→ ⑧
même	*same*	*very*	→ ⑨
pauvre	*poor (wretched)*	*poor (not rich)*	→ ⑩
propre	*own*	*clean*	→ ⑪
seul	*single, sole*	*on one's own*	→ ⑫
simple	*mere, simple*	*simple, easy*	→ ⑬
vrai	*real*	*true*	→ ⑭

Adjectives following the noun are linked by **et** → ⑮

1	**le chapitre suivant** the following chapter	**l'heure exacte** the right time
2	**une cravate rouge** a red tie	**un mot français** a French word
3	**ce dictionnaire** this dictionary	**mon père** my father
	le premier étage the first floor	**deux exemples** two examples
	quel homme? which man?	
4	**une autre fois** another time	**chaque jour** every day
5	**un ancien collègue** a former colleague	**l'histoire ancienne** ancient history
6	**un brave homme** a good man	**un homme brave** a brave man
7	**mes chers amis** my dear friends	**une robe chère** an expensive dress
8	**un grand peintre** a great painter	**un homme grand** a tall man
9	**la même réponse** the same answer	**vos paroles mêmes** your very words
10	**cette pauvre femme** that poor woman	**une nation pauvre** a poor nation
11	**ma propre vie** my own life	**une chemise propre** a clean shirt
12	**une seule réponse** a single reply	**une femme seule** a woman on her own
13	**un simple regard** a mere look	**un problème simple** a simple problem
14	**la vraie raison** the real reason	**les faits vrais** the true facts
15	**un acte lâche et trompeur** a cowardly, deceitful act	
	un acte lâche, trompeur et ignoble a cowardly, deceitful and ignoble act	

❑ Personal Pronouns

	SUBJECT PRONOUNS	
PERSON	SINGULAR	PLURAL
1st	**je (j')**	**nous**
	I	*we*
2nd	**tu**	**vous**
	you	*you*
3rd (masc.)	**il**	**ils**
	he; it	*they*
(fem.)	**elle**	**elles**
	she; it	*they*

je changes to **j'** before a vowel, an **h** 'mute', or the pronoun **y** → ①

◆ **tu/vous**

Vous, as well as being the second person plural, is also used when addressing one person. As a general rule, use **tu** only when addressing a friend, a child, a relative, someone you know very well, or when invited to do so. In all other cases use **vous**. For singular and plural uses of **vous**, see example ②

◆ **il/elle; ils/elles**

The form of the 3rd person pronouns reflects the number and gender of the noun(s) they replace, referring to animals and things as well as to people. **Ils** also replaces a combination of masculine and feminine nouns → ③

◆ Sometimes stressed pronouns replace the subject pronouns, see p 172.

1.   **J'arrive!**
I'm just coming!
J'en ai trois
I've got 3 of them
J'hésite à le déranger
I hesitate to disturb him
J'y pense souvent
I often think about it

2. Compare: **Vous êtes certain, Monsieur Leclerc?**
                Are you sure, Mr Leclerc?
  and: **Vous êtes certains, les enfants?**
                Are you sure, children?
  Compare: **Vous êtes partie quand, Estelle?**
                When did you leave, Estelle?
  and: **Estelle et Sophie – vous êtes parties
                quand?**
                Estelle and Sophie – when did you leave?

3. **Où logent ton père et ta mère quand ils vont à Rome?**
Where do your father and mother stay when they go to Rome?
Donne-moi le journal et les lettres quand ils arriveront
Give me the newspaper and the letters when they arrive

☐ **Personal Pronouns** (Continued)

	DIRECT OBJECT PRONOUNS	
PERSON	SINGULAR	PLURAL
1st	**me (m')**	**nous**
	me	*us*
2nd	**te (t')**	**vous**
	you	*you*
3rd (masc.)	**le (l')**	**les**
	him; it	*them*
(fem.)	**la (l')**	**les**
	her; it	*them*

The forms shown in brackets are used before a vowel, an **h** 'mute', or the pronoun **y** → 1

◆ In positive commands **me** and **te** change to **moi** and **toi** except before **en** or **y** → 2

◆ **le** sometimes functions as a 'neuter' pronoun, referring to an idea or information contained in a previous statement or question. It is often not translated → 3

Position of direct object pronouns

◆ In constructions other than the imperative affirmative the pronoun comes before the verb → 4

The same applies when the verb is in the infinitive → 5

In the imperative affirmative, the pronoun follows the verb and is attached to it by a hyphen → 6

◆ For further information, see Order of Object Pronouns, p 170.

Reflexive Pronouns

These are dealt with under reflexive verbs, p 30.

1. **Il m'a vu**
   He saw me
   Je ne t'oublierai jamais
   I'll never forget you
   Ça l'habitue à travailler seul
   That gets him/her used to working on his/her own
   Je veux l'y accoutumer
   I want to accustom him/her to it

2. **Avertis-moi de ta décision → Avertis-m'en**
   Inform me of your decision   Inform me of it

3. **Il n'est pas là. – Je le sais bien.**
   He isn't there. – I know that.
   Aidez-moi si vous le pouvez
   Help me if you can
   Elle viendra demain. – Je l'espère bien.
   She'll come tomorrow. – I hope so.

4. **Je t'aime**
   I love you
   Les voyez-vous?
   Can you see them?
   Elle ne nous connaît pas
   She doesn't know us
   Est-ce que tu ne les aimes pas?
   Don't you like them?
   Ne me faites pas rire
   Don't make me laugh

5. **Puis-je vous aider?**
   May I help you?

6. **Aidez-moi**   **Suivez-nous**
   Help me   Follow us

☐ **Personal Pronouns** *(Continued)*

	INDIRECT OBJECT PRONOUNS	
PERSON	SINGULAR	PLURAL
1st	**me (m')**	**nous**
2nd	**te (t')**	**vous**
3rd (masc.)	**lui**	**leur**
(fem.)	**lui**	**leur**

me and **te** change to **m'** and **t'** before a vowel or an **h** 'mute' → ①

- In positive commands, **me** and **te** change to **moi** and **toi** except before **en** → ②

- The pronouns shown in the above table replace the preposition **à** + noun, where the noun is a person or an animal → ③

- The verbal construction affects the translation of the pronoun → ④

Position of indirect object pronouns

- In constructions other than the imperative affirmative, the pronoun comes before the verb → ⑤
  The same applies when the verb is in the infinitive → ⑥
  In the imperative affirmative, the pronoun follows the verb and is attached to it by a hyphen → ⑦

- For further information, see Order of Object Pronouns, p 170.

Reflexive Pronouns

These are dealt with under reflexive verbs, p 30.

Examples

Grammar

1. **Tu m'as donné ce livre**
You gave me this book
Ils t'ont caché les faits
They hid the facts from you

2. **Donnez-moi du sucre** → **Donnez-m'en**
Give me some sugar   Give me some
Garde-toi assez d'argent → **Garde-t'en assez**
Keep enough money for   Keep enough for yourself
yourself

3. **J'écris à Suzanne** → **Je lui écris**
I'm writing to Suzanne   I'm writing to her
Donne du lait au chat → **Donne-lui du lait**
Give the cat some milk   Give it some milk

4. **arracher qch à qn**   to snatch sth from sb:
     Un voleur m'a arraché mon porte-monnaie
     A thief snatched my purse from me
promettre qch à qn   to promise sb sth:
     Il leur a promis un cadeau
     He promised them a present
demander à qn de faire   to ask sb to do:
     Elle nous avait demandé de revenir
     She had asked us to come back

5. **Elle vous a écrit**   **Vous a-t-elle écrit?**
She's written to you   Has she written to you?
Il ne nous parle pas
He doesn't speak to us
Est-ce que cela ne vous intéresse pas?
Doesn't it interest you?
Ne leur répondez pas
Don't answer them

6. **Voulez-vous leur envoyer l'adresse?**
Do you want to send them the address?

7. **Répondez-moi**   **Donnez-nous la réponse**
Answer me   Tell us the answer

◻ **Personal Pronouns** *(Continued)*

Order of object pronouns

+ When two object pronouns of different persons come before the verb, the order is: indirect before direct, i.e.

| me te nous vous | before | le la les | → 1 |

+ When two 3rd person object pronouns come before the verb, the order is: direct before indirect, i.e.

| le la les | before | lui leur | → 2 |

+ When two object pronouns come after the verb (i.e. in the imperative affirmative), the order is: direct before indirect, i.e.

| le la les | before | moi toi lui nous vous leur | → 3 |

+ The pronouns **y** and **en** (see pp 176 and 174) always come last → 4

1   **Dominique vous l'envoie demain**
Dominique's sending it to you tomorrow
Est-ce qu'il te les a montrés?
Has he shown them to you?
Ne me le dis pas
Don't tell me (it)
Il ne veut pas nous la prêter
He won't lend it to us

2   **Elle le leur a emprunté**
She borrowed it from them
Je les lui ai lus
I read them to him/her
Ne la leur donne pas
Don't give it to them
Je voudrais les lui rendre
I'd like to give them back to him/her

3   **Rends-les-moi**
Give them back to me
Donnez-le-nous
Give it to us
Apportons-les-leur
Let's take them to them

4   **Donnez-leur-en**
Give them some
Je l'y ai déposé
I dropped him there
Ne nous en parlez plus
Don't speak to us about it any more

☐ **Personal Pronouns** *(Continued)*

STRESSED OR DISJUNCTIVE PRONOUNS		
PERSON	SINGULAR	PLURAL
1st	**moi**	**nous**
	me	*us*
2nd	**toi**	**vous**
	you	*you*
3rd (masc.)	**lui**	**eux**
	him; it	*them*
(fem.)	**elle**	**elles**
	her; it	*them*
('reflexive')	**soi**	
	oneself	

◆ These pronouns are used:

  – after prepositions → 1
  – on their own → 2
  – following **c'est, ce sont** *it is* → 3
  – for emphasis, especially where contrast is involved → 4
  – when the subject consists of two or more pronouns → 5
  – when the subject consists of a pronoun and a noun → 6
  – in comparisons → 7
  – before relative pronouns → 8

◆ For particular emphasis **-même** (singular) or **-mêmes** (plural) is added to the pronoun → 9

moi-même	*myself*	**nous-mêmes**	*ourselves*
toi-même	*yourself*	**vous-même**	*yourself*
lui-même	*himself; itself*	**vous-mêmes**	*yourselves*
elle-même	*herself; itself*	**eux-mêmes**	*themselves*
soi-même	*oneself*	**elles-mêmes**	*themselves*

1. **Je pense à toi**   **Partez sans eux**
I think about you   Leave without them
C'est pour elle   **Assieds-toi à côté de lui**
This is for her   Sit beside him
Venez avec moi   **Il a besoin de nous**
Come with me   He needs us

2. **Qui a fait cela? – Lui.**
Who did that? – He did.
Qui est-ce qui gagne? – Moi
Who's winning? – Me

3. **C'est toi, Simon? – Non, c'est moi, David.**
Is that you, Simon? – No, it's me, David.
Qui est-ce? – Ce sont eux.
Who is it? – It's them.

4. **Ils voyagent séparément: lui par le train, elle en autobus**
They travel separately: he by train and she by bus
Toi, tu ressembles à ton père, eux pas
You look like your father, *they* don't
Il n'a pas l'air de s'ennuyer, lui!
He doesn't look bored!

5. **Lui et moi partons demain**
He and I are leaving tomorrow
Ni vous ni elles ne pouvez rester
Neither you nor they can stay

6. **Mon père et elle ne s'entendent pas**
My father and she don't get on

7. **plus jeune que moi**   **Il est moins grand que toi**
younger than me   He's smaller than you (are)

8. **Moi, qui étais malade, je n'ai pas pu les accompagner**
I, who was ill, couldn't go with them
Ce sont eux qui font du bruit, pas nous
They're the ones making the noise, not us

9. **Je l'ai fait moi-même**
I did it myself

❏ The pronoun en

◆ **en** replaces the preposition **de** + noun → ①
The verbal construction can affect the translation → ②

◆ **en** also replaces the partitive article *(English = some, any)* + noun → ③

In expressions of quantity **en** represents the noun → ④

◆ Position:

   en comes before the verb, except in positive commands when it follows and is attached to the verb by a hyphen → ⑤

◆ **en** follows other object pronouns → ⑥

1 **Il est fier de son succès** → **Il en est fier**
He's proud of his success   He's proud of it
Elle est sortie du cinéma → **Elle en est sortie**
She came out of the cinema   She came out (of it)
Je suis couvert de peinture → **J'en suis couvert**
I'm covered in paint   I'm covered in it
Il a beaucoup d'amis → **Il en a beaucoup**
He has lots of friends   He has lots (of them)

2 **avoir besoin de qch**   to need sth:
  J'en ai besoin
  I need it/them
avoir peur de qch   to be afraid of sth:
  J'en ai peur
  I'm afraid of it/them

3 **Avez-vous de l'argent?** → **En avez-vous?**
Have you any money?   Do you have any?
Je veux acheter des timbres → **Je veux en acheter**
I want to buy some stamps   I want to buy some

4 **J'ai deux crayons** → **J'en ai deux**
I've two pencils   I've two (of them)
Combien de sœurs as-tu? – J'en ai trois.
How many sisters do you have? – I have three.

5 **Elle en a discuté avec moi**
She discussed it with me
En êtes-vous content?
Are you pleased with it/them?
Je veux en garder trois
I want to keep three of them
N'en parlez plus
Don't talk about it any more
Prenez-en   **Soyez-en fier**
Take some   Be proud of it/them

6 **Donnez-leur-en**   **Il m'en a parlé**
Give them some   He spoke to me about it

❏ The pronoun y

- **y** replaces the preposition **à** + noun → ①
  The verbal construction can affect the translation → ②

- **y** also replaces the prepositions **dans** and **sur** + noun → ③

- **y** can also mean *there* → ④

- Position:
  y comes before the verb, except in positive commands when it
  follows and is attached to the verb by a hyphen → ⑤

- **y** follows other object pronouns → ⑥

☐1 **Ne touchez pas à ce bouton**   → **N'y touchez pas**
    Don't touch this switch   Don't touch it
    Il participe aux concerts   → **Il y participe**
    He takes part in the concerts   He takes part (in them)

☐2 **penser à qch**   to think about sth:
        J'y pense souvent
        I often think about it
    consentir à qch   to agree to sth:
        Tu y as consenti?
        Have you agreed to it?

☐3 **Mettez-les dans la boîte**   → **Mettez-les-y**
    Put them in the box   Put them in it
    Il les a mis sur les étagères   → **Il les y a mis**
    He put them on the shelves   He put them on them
    J'ai placé de l'argent sur ce   → **J'y ai placé de l'argent**
    compte   I've put money into it
    I've put money into this
    account

☐4 **Elle y passe tout l'été**
    She spends the whole summer there

☐5 **Il y a ajouté du sucre**
    He added sugar to it
    Elle n'y a pas écrit son nom
    She hasn't written her name on it
    Comment fait-on pour y aller?
    How do you get there?
    N'y pense plus!
    Don't give it another thought!
    Restez-y   **Réfléchissez-y**
    Stay there   Think it over

☐6 **Elle m'y a conduit**   **Menez-nous-y**
    She drove me there   Take us there

◻ Indefinite Pronouns

aucun(e)	*none, not any*	→ 1
certain(e)s	*some, certain*	→ 2
chacun(e)	*each (one)*	→ 3
	everybody	
on	*one, you*	
	somebody	→ 4
	they, people	
	we (informal use)	
personne	*nobody*	→ 5
plusieurs	*several*	→ 6
quelque chose	*something; anything*	→ 7
quelques-un(e)s	*some, a few*	→ 8
quelqu'un	*somebody; anybody*	→ 9
rien	*nothing*	→ 10
tout	*all; everything*	→ 11
tous (toutes)	*all*	→ 12
l'un(e) … l'autre	*(the) one … the other*	
les un(e)s … les autres	*some … others*	→ 13

♦ **aucun(e), personne, rien**

When used as subject or object of the verb, these require the word **ne** placed immediately before the verb. Note that **aucun** further needs the pronoun **en** when used as an object → 14

♦ **quelque chose, rien**

When qualified by an adjective, these pronouns require the preposition **de** before the adjective → 15

1	**Combien en avez-vous? – Aucun** How many have you got? – None	
2	**Certains pensent que ...** Some (people) think that ...	
3	**Chacune de ces boîtes est pleine** Each of these boxes is full	**Chacun son tour!** Everybody in turn!
4	**On voit l'église de cette fenêtre** You can see the church from this window **À la campagne on se couche tôt** In the country they/we go to bed early **Est-ce qu'on lui a permis de rester?** Was he/she allowed to stay?	
5	**Qui voyez-vous? – Personne** Who can you see? – Nobody	
6	**Ils sont plusieurs** There are several of them	
7	**Mange donc quelque chose!** Eat something!	**Tu as vu quelque chose?** Did you see anything?
8	**Je connais quelques-uns de ses amis** I know some of his/her friends	
9	**Quelqu'un a appelé** Somebody called (out)	**Tu as vu quelqu'un?** Did you see anybody?
10	**Qu'est-ce que tu as dans la main? – Rien** What have you got in your hand? – Nothing	
11	**Il a tout gâché** He has spoiled everything	**Tout va bien** All's well
12	**Tu les as tous?** Do you have all of them?	**Elles sont toutes venues** They all came
13	**Les uns sont satisfaits, les autres pas** Some are satisfied, (the) others aren't	
14	**Je ne vois personne** I can't see anyone **Aucune des entreprises ne veut ...** None of the companies wants ...	**Rien ne lui plaît** Nothing pleases him/her **Il n'en a aucun** He hasn't any (of them)
15	**quelque chose de grand** something big	**rien d'intéressant** nothing interesting

☐ Relative Pronouns

qui	*who; which*
que	*who(m); which*

These are subject and direct object pronouns that introduce a clause and refer to people or things.

	PEOPLE	THINGS
SUBJECT	**qui →** 1	**qui →** 3
	who, that	*which, that*
DIRECT	**que (qu') →** 2	**que (qu') →** 4
OBJECT	*who(m), that*	*which, that*

- **que** changes to **qu'** before a vowel → 2/4

- You cannot omit the object relative pronoun in French as you can in English → 2/4

After a preposition:
- When referring to people, use **qui** → 5
  EXCEPTIONS: after **parmi** *among* and **entre** *between* use **lesquels/lesquelles** (see below) → 6
- When referring to things, use forms of **lequel**:

	MASCULINE	FEMININE	
SING.	**lequel**	**laquelle**	*which*
PLUR.	**lesquels**	**lesquelles**	*which*

The pronoun agrees in number and gender with the noun → 7

- After the prepositions **à** and **de, lequel** and **lesquel(le)s** contract as follows:

  à + lequel → **auquel**
  à + lesquels → **auxquels**   → 8
  à + lesquelles → **auxquelles**

  de + lequel → **duquel**
  de + lesquels → **desquels**   → 9
  de + lesquelles → **desquelles**

1. **Mon frère, qui a vingt ans, est à l'université**
   My brother, who's twenty, is at university

2. **Les amis que je vois le plus sont ...**
   The friends (that) I see most are ...
   Lucienne, qu'il connaît depuis longtemps, est ...
   Lucienne, whom he has known for a long time, is ...

3. **Il y a un escalier qui mène au toit**
   There's a staircase which leads to the roof

4. **La maison que nous avons achetée a ...**
   The house (which) we've bought has ...
   Voici le cadeau qu'elle m'a envoyé
   This is the present (that) she sent me

5. **la personne à qui il parle**
   the person he's talking to
   la personne avec qui je voyage
   the person with whom I travel
   les enfants pour qui je l'ai acheté
   the children for whom I bought it

6. **Il y avait des jeunes, parmi lesquels Robert**
   There were some young people, Robert among them
   les filles entre lesquelles j'étais assis
   the girls between whom I was sitting

7. **le torchon avec lequel il l'essuie**
   the cloth he's wiping it with
   la table sur laquelle je l'ai mis
   the table on which I put it
   les moyens par lesquels il l'accomplit
   the means by which he achieves it
   les pièces pour lesquelles elle est connue
   the plays for which she is famous

8. **le magasin auquel il livre ces marchandises**
   the shop to which he delivers these goods

9. **les injustices desquelles il se plaint**
   the injustices he's complaining about

☐ **Relative Pronouns** *(Continued)*

quoi *which, what*

♦ When the relative pronoun does not refer to a specific noun, **quoi** is used after a preposition → 1

dont *whose, of whom, of which*

♦ **dont** often (but not always) replaces **de qui, duquel, de laquelle**, and **desquel(le)s** → 2

♦ It cannot replace **de qui, duquel** *etc* in the construction preposition + noun + **de qui/duquel** → 3

1. **C'est en quoi vous vous trompez**
   That's where you're wrong
   À quoi, j'ai répondu, '...'
   To which I replied, '...'

2. **la femme dont (= de qui) la voiture est garée en face**
   the woman whose car is parked opposite
   un prix dont (= de qui) je suis fier
   an award I am proud of
   un ami dont (= de qui) je connais le frère
   a friend whose brother I know
   les enfants dont (= de qui) vous vous occupez
   the children you look after
   le film dont (= duquel) il a parlé
   the film of which he spoke
   la fenêtre dont (= de laquelle) les rideaux sont tirés
   the window whose curtains are drawn
   des livres dont (= desquels) j'ai oublié les titres
   books whose titles I've forgotten
   les maladies dont (= desquelles) il souffre
   the illnesses he suffers from

3. **une personne sur l'aide de qui on peut compter**
   a person whose help one can rely on
   les enfants aux parents de qui j'écris
   the children to whose parents I'm writing
   la maison dans le jardin de laquelle il y a ...
   the house in whose garden there is ...

☐ **Relative Pronouns** *(Continued)*

ce qui, ce que   *that which, what*

These are used when the relative pronoun does not refer to a specific noun, and they are often translated as *what* (literally: *that which*)

> **ce qui**   is used as the subject → ☐1
>
> **ce que***   is used as the direct object → ☐2
>
> ***que** changes to **qu'** before a vowel → ☐2

◆ Note the construction

> **tout ce qui** ⎫
> **tout ce que** ⎬   *everything/all that* → ☐3

◆ **de + ce que → ce dont** → ☐4

◆ preposition + **ce que → ce** + preposition + **quoi** → ☐5

◆ When **ce qui, ce que** *etc*, refers to a previous CLAUSE the translation is *which* → ☐6

1   **Ce qui m'intéresse ne l'intéresse pas forcément**
What interests me doesn't necessarily interest him
Je n'ai pas vu ce qui s'est passé
I didn't see what happened

2   **Ce que j'aime c'est la musique classique**
What I like is classical music
Montrez-moi ce qu'il vous a donné
Show me what he gave you

3   **Tout ce qui reste c'est …**
All that's left is …
Donnez-moi tout ce que vous avez
Give me everything you have

4   **Il risque de perdre ce dont il est si fier**
He risks losing what he's so proud of
Voilà ce dont il s'agit
That's what it's about

5   **Ce n'est pas ce à quoi je m'attendais**
It's not what I was expecting
Ce à quoi je m'intéresse particulièrement c'est …
What I'm particularly interested in is …

6   **Il est d'accord, ce qui m'étonne**
He agrees, which surprises me
Il a dit qu'elle ne venait pas, ce que nous savions déjà
He said she wasn't coming, which we already knew

◻ Interrogative Pronouns

qui?	*who; whom?*
que?	*what?*
quoi?	*what?*

These pronouns are used in direct questions.

The form of the pronoun depends on:
- whether it refers to people or to things
- whether it is the subject or object of the verb, or if it comes after a preposition

Qui and **que** have longer forms, as shown in the tables below.

♦ Referring to people:

SUBJECT	**qui?**	
	qui est-ce qui?	→ 1
	who?	
OBJECT	**qui?**	
	qui est-ce que*?	→ 2
	who(m)?	
AFTER PREPOSITIONS	**qui?**	→ 3
	who(m)?	

♦ Referring to things:

SUBJECT	**qu'est-ce qui?**	→ 4
	what?	
OBJECT	**que*?**	
	qu'est-ce que*?	→ 5
	what?	
AFTER PREPOSITIONS	**quoi?**	→ 6
	what?	

*****que** changes to **qu'** before a vowel → 2, 5

1   **Qui vient?**
       Qui est-ce qui vient?
       Who's coming?

2   **Qui vois-tu?**
       Qui est-ce que tu vois?
       Who(m) can you see?
       Qui a-t-elle rencontré?
       Qui est-ce qu'elle a rencontré?
       Who(m) did she meet?

3   **De qui parle-t-il?**
       Who's he talking about?
       Pour qui est ce livre?
       Who's this book for?
       À qui avez-vous écrit?
       To whom did you write?

4   **Qu'est-ce qui se passe?**
       What's happening?
       Qu'est-ce qul a vexé Paul?
       What upset Paul?

5   **Que faites-vous?**
       Qu'est-ce que vous faites?
       What are you doing?
       Qu'a-t-il dit?
       Qu'est-ce qu'il a dit?
       What did he say?

6   **À quoi cela sert-il?**
       What's that used for?
       De quoi a-t-on parlé?
       What was the discussion about?
       Sur quoi vous basez-vous?
       What do you base it on?

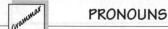

□ **Interrogative Pronouns** *(Continued)*

qui	*who; whom*
ce qui	*what*
ce que	*what*
quoi	*what*

These pronouns are used in indirect questions.
The form of the pronoun depends on:
- whether it refers to people or to things
- whether it is the subject or object of the verb, or if it comes after a preposition

- Referring to people: use **qui** in all instances → 1

- Referring to things:

SUBJECT	**ce qui**	→ 2
	what	
OBJECT	**ce que***	→ 3
	what	
AFTER	**quoi**	→ 4
PREPOSITIONS	*what*	

***que** changes to **qu'** before a vowel → 3

1 **Demande-lui qui est venu**
Ask him who came
Je me demande qui ils ont vu
I wonder who they saw
Dites-moi qui vous préférez
Tell me who you prefer
Elle ne sait pas à qui s'adresser
She doesn't know who to apply to
Demandez-leur pour qui elles travaillent
Ask them who they work for

2 **Il se demande ce qui se passe**
He's wondering what's happening
Je ne sais pas ce qui vous fait croire que ...
I don't know what makes you think that ...

3 **Raconte-nous ce que tu as fait**
Tell us what you did
Je me demande ce qu'elle pense
I wonder what she's thinking

4 **On ne sait pas de quoi vivent ces animaux**
We don't know what these animals live on
Je vais lui demander à quoi il fait allusion
I'm going to ask him what he's hinting at

◻ **Interrogative Pronouns** *(Continued)*

lequel?, laquelle?; lesquels?, lesquelles?

	MASCULINE	FEMININE	
SING.	**lequel?**	**laquelle?**	*which (one)?*
PLUR.	**lesquels?**	**lesquelles?**	*which (ones)?*

- The pronoun agrees in number and gender with the noun it refers to → ①

- The same forms are used in indirect questions → ②

- After the prepositions **à** and **de**, **lequel** and **lesquel(le)s** contract as follows:

  à + lequel? → auquel?
  à + lesquels? → auxquels?
  à + lesquelles? → auxquelles?

  de + lequel? → duquel?
  de + lesquels? → desquels?
  de + lesquelles? → desquelles?

1. **J'ai choisi un livre. – Lequel?**
   I've chosen a book. – Which one?
   Laquelle de ces valises est la vôtre?
   Which of these cases is yours?
   Amenez quelques amis. – Lesquels?
   Bring some friends. – Which ones?
   Lesquelles de vos sœurs sont mariées?
   Which of your sisters are married?

2. **Je me demande laquelle des maisons est la leur**
   I wonder which is their house
   Dites-moi lesquels d'entre eux étaient là
   Tell me which of them were there

◻ Possessive Pronouns

SINGULAR		
MASCULINE	FEMININE	
le mien	**la mienne**	*mine*
le tien	**la tienne**	*yours*
le sien	**la sienne**	*his; hers; its*
le nôtre	**la nôtre**	*ours*
le vôtre	**la vôtre**	*yours*
le leur	**la leur**	*theirs*

PLURAL		
MASCULINE	FEMININE	
les miens	**les miennes**	*mine*
les tiens	**les tiennes**	*yours*
les siens	**les siennes**	*his; hers; its*
les nôtres	**les nôtres**	*ours*
les vôtres	**les vôtres**	*yours*
les leurs	**les leurs**	*theirs*

- The pronoun agrees in number and gender with the noun it replaces, NOT WITH THE OWNER → ⊡

- Alternative translations are *my own, your own* etc; **le sien, la sienne** etc may also mean *one's own* → ②

- After the prepositions **à** and **de** the articles **le** and **les** are contracted in the normal way (see p 140):

à + le mien → au mien
à + les miens → aux miens   → ③
à + les miennes → aux miennes

de + le mien → du mien
de + les miens → des miens   → ④
de + les miennes → des miennes

1

Demandez à Carole si ce stylo est le sien
Ask Carole if this pen is hers

Quelle équipe a gagné – la leur ou la nôtre?
Which team won – theirs or ours?

Mon stylo marche mieux que le tien
My pen writes better than yours

Richard a pris mes affaires pour les siennes
Richard mistook my belongings for his

Si tu n'as pas de disques, emprunte les miens
If you don't have any records, borrow mine

Nos maisons sont moins grandes que les vôtres
Our houses are smaller than yours

2

Est-ce que leur entreprise est aussi grande que la vôtre?
Is their company as big as your own?

Leurs prix sont moins élevés que les nôtres
Their prices are lower than our own

Le bonheur des autres importe plus que le sien
Other people's happiness matters more than one's own

3

Pourquoi préfères-tu ce manteau au mien?
Why do you prefer this coat to mine?

Quelles maisons ressemblent aux leurs?
Which houses resemble theirs?

4

Leur car est garé
Their coach is parked

Vos livres sont au-dessus des miens
Your books are on top of mine

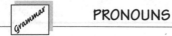
◻ Demonstrative Pronouns

celui, celle; ceux, celles

	MASCULINE	FEMININE	
SING.	**celui**	**celle**	*the one*
PLUR.	**ceux**	**celles**	*the ones*

- The pronoun agrees in number and gender with the noun it replaces
  → 1

- Uses:

  - preceding a relative pronoun, meaning *the one(s) who/which* → 1
  - preceding the preposition **de**, meaning *the one(s) belonging to, the one(s) of* → 2
  - with **-ci** and **-là**, for emphasis or to distinguish between two things:

	MASCULINE	FEMININE		
SING.	**celui-ci**	**celle-ci**	*this (one)*	→ 3
PLUR.	**ceux-ci**	**celles-ci**	*these (ones)*	

	MASCULINE	FEMININE		
SING.	**celui-là**	**celle-là**	*that(one)*	→ 3
PLUR.	**ceux-là**	**celles-là**	*those (ones)*	

  - an additional meaning of **celui-ci/celui-là** *etc* is *the former/the latter*.

1. **Lequel? – Celui qui parle à Anne**
   Which man? – The one who's talking to Anne
   Quelle robe désirez-vous? – Celle qui est en vitrine
   Which dress do you want? – The one which is in the window
   Est-ce que ces livres sont ceux qu'il t'a donnés?
   Are these the books that he gave you?
   Quelles filles? – Celles que nous avons vues hier
   Which girls? – The ones we saw yesterday
   Cet article n'est pas celui dont vous m'avez parlé
   This article isn't the one you spoke to me about

2. **Ce jardin est plus grand que celui de mes parents**
   This garden is bigger than my parents' (garden)
   Est-ce que ta fille est plus âgée que celle de Gabrielle?
   Is your daughter older than Gabrielle's (daughter)?
   Je préfère les enfants de Paul à ceux de Roger
   I prefer Paul's children to Roger's (children)
   Comparez vos réponses à celles de votre voisin
   Compare your answers with your neighbour's (answers)
   les montagnes d'Écosse et celles du pays de Galles
   the mountains of Scotland and those of Wales

3. **Quel tailleur préférez-vous: celui-ci ou celui-là?**
   Which suit do you prefer: this one or that one?
   Cette chemise a deux poches mais celle-là n'en a pas
   This shirt has two pockets but that one has none
   Quels œufs choisirais-tu: ceux-ci ou ceux-là?
   Which eggs would you choose: these (ones) or those (ones)?
   De toutes mes jupes, celle-ci me va le mieux
   Of all my skirts, this one fits me best

□ **Demonstrative Pronouns** *(Continued)*

ce (c')   *it, that*

+ Usually used with **être**, in the expressions **c'est, c'était, ce sont** *etc*
  → 1

+ Note the spelling **ç** when followed by the letter **a** → 2

+ Uses:
  – to identify a person or object → 3
  – for emphasis → 4
  – as a neuter pronoun, referring to a statement, idea *etc* → 5

ce qui, ce que, ce dont etc: see Relative Pronouns (p 184),
Interrogative Pronouns (p 188).

cela, ça   *it, that*

+ **cela** and **ça** are used as 'neuter' pronouns, referring to a statement,
  an idea, an object → 6

+ In everyday spoken language **ça** is used in preference to **cela**

ceci   *this* → 7

+ **ceci** is not used as often as 'this' in English; **cela**, **ça** are often used
  where we use 'this'.

1. **C'est ...**   **C'était moi**
   It's/That's ...   It was me

2. **Ç'a été la cause de ...**
   It has been the cause of...

3. **Qui est-ce?**
   Who is it?; Who's this/that?; Who's he/she?
   C'est lui/mon frère/nous   **Ce sont eux**
   It's/That's him/my brother/us   It's them
   C'est une infirmière*   **Ce sont des professeurs***
   She's a nurse   They're teachers
   Qu'est-ce que c'est?   **Qu'est-ce que c'est que ça?**
   What's this/that?   What's that?
   C'est une agrafeuse   **Ce sont des trombones**
   It's a stapler   They're paper clips

4. **C'est moi qui ai téléphoné**
   It was me who phoned
   Ce sont les enfants qui importent le plus
   It's the children who matter most

5. **C'est très intéressant**
   That's/It's very interesting
   Ce serait dangereux
   That/It would be dangerous

6. **Ça ne fait rien**
   It doesn't matter
   À quoi bon faire ça?
   What's the use of doing that?
   Cela ne compte pas
   That doesn't count
   Cela demande du temps
   It/That takes time

7. **À qui est ceci?**   **Ouvrez-le comme ceci**
   Whose is this?   Open it like this

*See pp 146 and 147 for the use of the article when stating a person's profession

⌐ Adverbs

Formation

- Most adverbs are formed by adding **-ment** to the feminine form of the adjective → 1

- **-ment** is added to the *masculine* form when the masculine form ends in **-é**, **-i** or **-u** → 2

  EXCEPTION: **gai** → 3

  Occasionally the **u** changes to **û** before **-ment** is added → 4

- If the adjective ends in **-ant** or **-ent**, the adverb ends in **-amment** or **-emment** → 5

  EXCEPTIONS: **lent, présent** → 6

Irregular Adverbs

ADJECTIVE		ADVERB		
aveugle	*blind*	**aveuglément**	blindly	
bon	*good*	**bien**	well	→ 7
bref	*brief*	**brièvement**	briefly	
énorme	*enormous*	**énormément**	enormously	
exprès	*express*	**expressément**	expressly	→ 8
gentil	*kind*	**gentiment**	kindly	
mauvais	*bad*	**mal**	badly	→ 9
meilleur	*better*	**mieux**	better	
pire	*worse*	**pis**	worse	
précis	*precise*	**précisément**	precisely	
profond	*deep*	**profondément**	deeply	→ 10
traître	*treacherous*	**traîtreusement**	treacherously	

Adjectives used as adverbs

Certain adjectives are used adverbially. These include: **bas, bon, cher, clair, court, doux, droit, dur, faux, ferme, fort, haut, mauvais** and **net** → 11

1 MASC./FEM. ADJECTIVE	ADVERB
heureux/heureuse fortunate	**heureusement** fortunately
franc/franche frank	**franchement** frankly
extrême/extrême extreme	**extrêmement** extremely
2 MASC. ADJECTIVE	ADVERB
désespéré desperate	**désespérément** desperately
vrai true	**vraiment** truly
résolu resolute	**résolument** resolutely
3 **gai** cheerful	**gaiement** OR **gaîment** cheerfully
4 **continu** continuous	**continûment** continuously
5 **constant** constant	**constamment** constantly
courant fluent	**couramment** fluently
évident obvious	**évidemment** obviously
fréquent frequent	**fréquemment** frequently
6 **lent** slow	**lentement** slowly
présent present	**présentement** presently

7 **Elle travaille bien**
She works well

8 **Il a expressément défendu qu'on parte**
He has expressly forbidden us to leave

9 **Un emploi mal payé**
A badly paid job

10 **J'ai été profondément ému**
I was deeply moved

11 **parler bas/haut**
to speak softly/loudly
coûter cher
to be expensive
voir clair
to see clearly
travailler dur
to work hard
chanter faux
to sing off key
sentir bon/mauvais
to smell nice/horrible

❑ Position of Adverbs

- When the adverb accompanies a verb in a simple tense, it generally follows the verb → ①

- When the adverb accompanies a verb in a compound tense, it generally comes between the auxiliary verb and the past participle → ②

  Some adverbs, however, follow the past participle → ③

- When the adverb accompanies an adjective or another adverb it generally precedes the adjective/adverb → ④

❑ Comparatives of Adverbs

These are formed using the following constructions:

plus ... (que)	*more ... (than)*	→ ⑤
moins ... (que)	*less ... (than)*	→ ⑥
aussi ... que	*as ... as* → ⑦	
si ... que*	*as ... as* → ⑧	

*used mainly after a negative

❑ Superlatives of Adverbs

These are formed using the following constructions:

| **le plus ... (que)** | *the most ... (that)* → ⑨ |
| **le moins ... (que)** | *the least ... (that)* → ⑩ |

Adverbs with irregular comparatives/superlatives

ADVERB	COMPARATIVE	SUPERLATIVE
beaucoup	**plus**	**le plus**
a lot	*more*	*(the) most*
bien	**mieux**	**le mieux**
well	*better*	*(the) best*
mal	**pis** OR **plus mal**	**le pis** OR **le plus mal**
badly	*worse*	*(the) worst*
peu	**moins**	**le moins**
little	*less*	*(the) least*

1. **Il dort encore**
He's still asleep

   Je pense souvent à toi
I often think about you

2. **Ils sont déjà partis**
They've already gone

   J'ai presque fini
I'm almost finished

   J'ai toujours cru que ...
I've always thought that ...

   Il a trop mangé
He's eaten too much

3. **On les a vus partout**
We saw them everywhere

   Elle est revenue hier
She came back yesterday

4. **un très beau chemisier**
a very nice blouse

   une femme bien habillée
a well-dressed woman

   beaucoup plus vite
much faster

   peu souvent
not very often

5. **plus vite**
more quickly

   plus régulièrement
more regularly

   Elle chante plus fort que moi
She sings louder than I do

6. **moins facilement**
less easily

   moins souvent
less often

   Nous nous voyons moins fréquemment qu'auparavant
We see each other less frequently than before

7. **Faites-le aussi vite que possible**
Do it as quickly as possible

   Il en sait aussi long que nous
He knows as much about it as we do

8. **Ce n'est pas si loin que je pensais**
It's not as far as I thought

9. **Marianne court le plus vite**
Marianne runs fastest

   Le plus tôt que je puisse venir c'est samedi
The earliest that I can come is Saturday

10. **C'est l'auteur que je connais le moins bien**
It's the writer I'm least familiar with

◻ Common adverbs and their usage

assez	*enough; quite*	→ 1 See also below
aussi	*also, too; as*	→ 2
autant	*as much*	→ 3 See also below
beaucoup	*a lot; much*	→ 4 See also below
bien	*well; very*	→ 5 See also below
	very much; 'indeed'	
combien	*how much; how many*	→ 6 See also below
comme	*how; what*	→ 7
déjà	*already; before*	→ 8
encore	*still; yet*	→ 9
	more; even	
moins	*less*	→ 10 See also below
peu	*little, not much; not very*	→ 11 See also below
plus	*more*	→ 12 See also below
si	*so; such*	→ 13
tant	*so much*	→ 14 See also below
toujours	*always; still*	→ 15
trop	*too much; too*	→ 16 See also below

+ **assez, autant, beaucoup, combien** *etc* are used in the construction adverb + **de** + noun with the following meanings:

assez de	*enough*	→ 17
autant de	*as much; as many*	
	so much; so many	
beaucoup de	*a lot of*	
combien de	*how much; how many*	
moins de	*less; fewer*	→ 17
peu de	*little, not much; few, not many*	
plus de	*more*	
tant de	*so much; so many*	
trop de	*too much; too many*	

+ **bien** can be followed by a partitive article (see p 144) plus a noun to mean *a lot of; a good many* → 18

1. **Avez-vous assez chaud?**
Are you warm enough?
   Il est assez tard
It's quite late

2. **Je préfère ça aussi**
I prefer it too
   Elle est aussi grande que moi
She is as tall as I am

3. **Je voyage autant que lui**
I travel as much as him

4. **Tu lis beaucoup?**
Do you read a lot?
   C'est beaucoup plus loin?
Is it much further?

5. **Bien joué!**
Well played!
   Je suis bien content que …
I'm very pleased that …
   Il s'est bien amusé
He enjoyed himself very much
   Je l'ai bien fait
I DID do it

6. **Combien coûte ce livre?**
How much is this book?
   Vous êtes combien?
How many of you are there?

7. **Comme tu es jolie!**
How pretty you look!
   Comme il fait beau!
What lovely weather!

8. **Je l'ai déjà fait**
I've already done it
   Êtes-vous déjà allé en France?
Have you been to France before?

9. **J'en ai encore deux**
I've still got two
   Elle n'est pas encore là
She isn't there yet
   Encore du café, Alain?
More coffee, Alan?
   Encore mieux!
Even better!

10. **Travaillez moins**
Work less
   Je suis moins étonné que toi
I'm less surprised than you are

11. **Elle mange peu**
She doesn't eat very much
   C'est peu important
It's not very important

12. **Il se détend plus**
He relaxes more
   Elle est plus timide que Sophie
She is shyer than Sophie

13. **Simon est si charmant**
Simon is so charming
   une si belle vue
such a lovely view

14. **Elle l'aime tant**
She loves him so much

15. **Il dit toujours ça!**
He always says that!
   Tu le vois toujours?
Do you still see him?

16. **J'ai trop mangé**
I've eaten too much
   C'est trop cher
It's too expensive

17. **assez d'argent/de livres**
enough money/books
   moins de temps/d'amis
less time/fewer friends

18. **bien du mal/des gens**
a lot of harm/a good many people

On the following pages you will find some of the most frequent uses of prepositions in French. Particular attention is paid to cases where usage differs markedly from English. It is often difficult to give an English equivalent for French prepositions, since usage *does* vary so much between the two languages.

In the list below, the broad meaning of the preposition is given on the left, with examples of usage following.

Prepositions are dealt with in alphabetical order, except **à**, **de** and **en** which are shown first.

à

at	**lancer qch à qn**	*to throw sth at sb*
	il habite à St. Pierre	*he lives at St. Pierre*
	à 5 francs (la) pièce	*(at) 5 francs each*
	à 100 km à l'heure	*at 100 km per hour*
in	**à la campagne**	*in the country*
	à Londres	*in London*
	au lit	*in bed (also* to bed*)*
	un livre à la main	*with a book in his/her hand*
on	**un tableau au mur**	*a picture on the wall*
to	**aller au cinéma**	*to go to the cinema*
	donner qch à qn	*to give sth to sb*
	le premier/dernier à faire	*the first/last to do*
	demander qch à qn	*to ask sb sth*
from	**arracher qch à qn**	*to snatch sth from sb*
	acheter qch à qn	*to buy sth from sb*
	cacher qch à qn	*to hide sth from sb*
	emprunter qch à qn	*to borrow sth from sb*
	prendre qch à qn	*to take sth from sb*
	voler qch à qn	*to steal sth from sb*

descriptive	**la femme au chapeau vert**	*the woman with the green hat*
	un garçon aux yeux bleus	*a boy with blue eyes*
manner, means	**à l'anglaise**	*in the English manner*
	fait à la main	*handmade*
	à bicyclette/cheval	*by bicycle/on horseback* (BUT note other forms of transport used with **en** and **par**)
	à pied	*on foot*
	chauffer au gaz	*to heat with/by gas*
	à pas lents	*with slow steps*
	cuisiner au beurre	*to cook with butter*
time, date: *at, in*	**à minuit**	*at midnight*
	à trois heures cinq	*at five past three*
	au 20ème siècle	*in the 20th century*
	à Noël/Pâques	*at Christmas/Easter*
distance	**à 6 km d'ici**	*(at a distance of) 6 km from here*
	à deux pas de chez moi	*just a step from my place*
destined for	**une tasse à thé**	*a teacup* (compare **une tasse de thé**, p 206)
	un service à café	*a coffee service*
after certain adjectives	**son écriture est difficile à lire**	*his writing is difficult to read* (compare the usage with **de**, p 206)
	prêt à tout	*ready for anything*
after certain verbs	see p 64	

de

from	**venir de Londres**	*to come from London*
	du matin au soir	*from morning till night*
	du 21 juin au 5 juillet	*from 21st June till 5th July*
	de 10 à 15	*from 10 to 15*
belonging to, of	**un ami de la famille**	*a family friend*
	les vents d'automne	*the autumn winds*
contents, composition, material	**une boîte d'allumettes**	*a box of matches*
	une tasse de thé	*a cup of tea (compare* **une tasse à thé**, *p 205)*
	une robe de soie	*a silk dress*
manner	**d'une façon irrégulière**	*in an irregular way*
	d'un coup de couteau	*with the blow of a knife*
quality	**la société de consommation**	*the consumer society*
	des objets de valeur	*valuable items*
comparative + a number	**il y avait plus/moins de cent personnes**	*there were more/fewer than a hundred people*
after superlatives: *in*	**la plus/moins belle ville du monde**	*the most/least beautiful city in the world*
after certain adjectives	**surpris de voir**	*surprised to see*
	il est difficile d'y accéder	*access is difficult (compare the usage with* **à**, *p 205)*
after certain verbs	see p 64	

en

place: *to, in, on*	**en ville**	*in/to town*
	en pleine mer	*on the open sea*
	en France	*in/to France* (note that masculine countries use **à**)
dates, months: *in*	**en 1923**	*in 1923*
	en janvier	*in January*
transport	**en voiture**	*by car*
	en avion	*by plane* (but note usage of **à** and **par** in other expressions)
language	**en français**	*in French*
duration	**je le ferai en trois jours**	*I'll do it in three days* (i.e. *I'll take 3 days to do it:* compare **dans trois jours**, p 208)
material	**un bracelet en or**	*a bracelet made of gold* (note that the use of **en** stresses the material more than the use of **de**)
	consister en	*to consist of*
in the manner of, like a	**parler en vrai connaisseur**	*to speak like a real connoisseur*
	déguisé en cowboy	*dressed up as a cowboy*
+ present participle	**il l'a vu en passant devant la porte**	*he saw it as he came past the door*

avant

before	**il est arrivé avant toi**	*he arrived before you*
+ infinitive (add **de**)	**je vais finir ça avant de manger**	*I'm going to finish this before eating*
preference	**la santé avant tout**	*health above all things*

chez

at the home of	**chez lui/moi**	*at his/my house*
	être chez soi	*to be at home*
	venez chez nous	*come round to our place*
at/to a shop	**chez le boucher**	*at/to the butcher's*
in a person, among a group of people or animals	**ce que je n'aime pas chez lui c'est son ...**	*what I don't like in him is his ...*
	chez les fourmis	*among ants*

dans

position	**dans une boîte**	*in(to) a box*
circumstance	**dans son enfance**	*in his childhood*
future time	**dans trois jours**	*in three days' time (compare **en trois jours**, p 207)*

depuis

since: time	**depuis mardi**	*since Tuesday*
place	**il pleut depuis Paris**	*it's been raining since Paris*
for	**il habite cette maison depuis 3 ans**	*he's been living in this house for 3 years* (NOTE TENSE)

dès

past time	**dès mon enfance**	*since my childhood*
future time	**je le ferai dès mon retour**	*I'll do it as soon as I get back*

entre

between	**entre 8 et 10**	*between 8 and 10*
among	**Jean et Pierre, entre autres**	*Jean and Pierre, among others*
reciprocal	**s'aider entre eux**	*to help each other (out)*

d'entre

of, among	**trois d'entre eux**	*three of them*

par

agent of passive: *by*	**renversé par une voiture**	*knocked down by a car*
	tué par la foudre	*killed by lightning*
weather conditions	**par un beau jour d'été**	*on a lovely summer's day*
by (means of)	**par un couloir/ sentier**	*by a corridor/path*
	par le train	*by train (but see also* **à** *and* **en**)
	par l'intermédiaire de M. Duval	*through Mr Duval*
distribution	**deux par deux**	*two by two*
	par groupes de dix	*in groups of ten*
	deux fois par jour	*twice a day*

pour

for	c'est pour vous	*it's for you*
	c'est pour demain	*it's for tomorrow*
	une chambre pour 2 nuits	*a room for 2 nights*
	pour un enfant, il se débrouille bien	*for a child he manages very well*
	il part pour l'Espagne	*he's leaving for Spain*
	il l'a fait pour vous	*he did it for you*
	il lui a donné 50 francs pour ce livre	*he gave him 50 francs for this book*
	je ne suis pas pour cette idée	*I'm not for that idea*
	pour qui me prends-tu?	*who do you take me for?*
	il passe pour un idiot	*he's taken for a fool*
+ infinitive: (in order) to	elle se pencha pour le ramasser	*she bent down to pick it up*
	c'est trop fragile pour servir de siège	*it's too fragile to be used as a seat*
to(wards)	être bon/gentil pour qn	*to be kind to sb*
with prices, time	pour 200 francs d'essence	*200 francs' worth of petrol*
	j'en ai encore pour une heure	*I'll be another hour (at it) yet*

sans

without	sans eau	*without water*
	sans ma femme	*without my wife*
+ infinitive	sans compter les autres	*without counting the others*

sauf

except (for)	**tous sauf lui**	*all except him*
	sauf quand il pleut	*except when it's raining*
barring	**sauf imprévu**	*barring the unexpected*
	sauf avis contraire	*unless you hear to the contrary*

sur

on	**sur le siège**	*on the seat*
	sur l'armoire	*on top of the wardrobe*
	sur le mur	*on (top of) the wall (if the meaning is hanging on the wall use à, p 204)*
	sur votre gauche	*on your left*
	être sur le point de faire	*to be on the point of doing*
on (to)	**mettez-le sur la table**	*put it on the table*
proportion: out of, by	**8 sur 10**	*8 out of 10*
	un automobiliste sur 5	*one motorist in 5*
	la pièce fait 2 mètres sur 3	*the room measures 2 metres by 3*

◻ Conjunctions

There are conjunctions which introduce a main clause, such as **et** *and*, **mais** *but*, **si** *if*, **ou** *or* etc, and those which introduce subordinate clauses like **parce que** *because*, **pendant que** *while*, **après que** *after* etc. They are all used in much the same way as in English, but the following points are of note:

- Some conjunctions in French require a following subjunctive, see p 58

- Some conjunctions are 'split' in French like *both ... and*, *either ... or* in English:

et ... et	*both ... and*	→ 1
ni ... ni ... ne	*neither ... nor*	→ 2
ou (bien) ... ou (bien)	*either ... or (else)*	→ 3
soit ... soit	*either ... or*	→ 4

- **si** + **il(s)** → **s'il(s)** → 5

- **que**
  – meaning *that* → 6
  – replacing another conjunction → 7
  – replacing **si**, see p 62
  – in comparisons, meaning *as, than* → 8
  – followed by the subjunctive, see p 62

- **aussi** *so, therefore*: the subject and verb are inverted if the subject is a pronoun → 9

① **Ces fleurs poussent et en été et en hiver**
These flowers grow in both summer and winter

② **Ni lui ni elle ne sont venus**
Neither he nor she came

Ils n'ont ni argent ni nourriture
They have neither money nor food

③ **Elle doit être ou naïve ou stupide**
She must be either naïve or stupid

Ou bien il m'évite ou bien il ne me reconnaît pas
Either he's avoiding me or else he doesn't recognize me

④ **Il faut choisir soit l'un soit l'autre**
You have to choose either one or the other

⑤ **Je ne sais pas s'il vient/s'ils viennent**
I don't know if he's coming/if they're coming

Dis-moi s'il y a des erreurs
Tell me if there are any mistakes

Votre passeport, s'il vous plaît
Your passport, please

⑥ **Il dit qu'il t'a vu**
He says (that) he saw you

Est-ce qu'elle sait que vous êtes là?
Does she know that you're here?

⑦ **Quand tu seras plus grand et que tu auras une maison à toi, ...**
When you're older and you have a house of your own, ...

Comme il pleuvait et que je n'avais pas de parapluie, ...
As it was raining and I didn't have an umbrella, ...

⑧ **Ils n'y vont pas aussi souvent que nous**
They don't go there as often as we do

Il les aime plus que jamais
He likes them more than ever

L'argent est moins lourd que le plomb
Silver is lighter than lead

⑨ **Ceux-ci sont plus rares, aussi coûtent-ils cher**
These ones are rarer, so they're expensive

◻ Word Order

Word order in French is largely the same as in English, except for the following. Most of these have already been dealt with under the appropriate part of speech, but are summarized here along with other instances not covered elsewhere.

- Object pronouns nearly always come before the verb → 1
  For details, see pp 166 to 170

- Certain adjectives come after the noun → 2
  For details, see p 162

- Adverbs accompanying a verb in a simple tense usually follow the verb → 3
  For details, see p 200

- After **aussi** *so, therefore*, **à peine** *hardly*, **peut-être** *perhaps*, the verb and subject are inverted → 4

- After the relative pronoun **dont** *whose* → 5
  For details, see p 182

- In exclamations, **que** and **comme** do not affect the normal word order → 6

- Following direct speech:
  - the *verb + subject* order is inverted to become *subject + verb* → 7
  - with a pronoun subject, the verb and pronoun are linked by a hyphen → 8
  - when the verb ends in a vowel in the 3rd person singular, **-t-** is inserted between the pronoun and the verb → 9

For word order in negative sentences, see p 216.
For word order in interrogative sentences, see pp 220 and 222.

1. **Je les vois!**   **Il me l'a donné**
   I can see them!   He gave it to me

2. **une ville française**   **du vin rouge**
   a French town   some red wine

3. **Il pleut encore**   **Elle m'aide quelquefois**
   It's still raining   She sometimes helps me

4. **Il vit tout seul, aussi fait-il ce qu'il veut**
   He lives alone, so he does what he likes
   À peine la pendule avait-elle sonné trois heures que ...
   Hardly had the clock struck three when ...
   Peut-être avez-vous raison
   Perhaps you're right

5. Compare: **un homme dont je connais la fille**
                   a man whose daughter I know
   and: **un homme dont la fille me connaît**
                   a man whose daughter knows me
   If the person (or object) 'owned' is the *object* of the verb, the order is:
   dont + verb + noun (1st sentence)
   If the person (or object) 'owned' is the *subject* of the verb, the order is:
   dont + noun + verb (2nd sentence)
   Note also: **l'homme dont elle est la fille**
                   the man whose daughter she is

6. **Qu'il fait chaud!**   **Que je suis content de vous voir!**
   How warm it is!   How pleased I am to see you!
   Comme c'est cher   **Que tes voisins sont gentils!**
   How expensive it is!   How kind your neighbours are!

7. **'Je pense que oui' a dit Luc**   **'Ça ne fait rien' répondit Jean**
   ' I think so', said Luke   'It doesn't matter', John replied

8. **'Quelle horreur!' me suis-je exclamé**
   'How awful!' I exclaimed

9. **'Pourquoi pas?' a-t-elle demandé**
   'Why not?' she asked
   'Si c'est vrai', continua-t-il '...'
   'If it's true', he went on '...'

◻ Negatives

ne ... pas	*not*
ne ... point (literary)	*not*
ne ... rien	*nothing*
ne ... personne	*nobody*
ne ... plus	*no longer, no more*
ne ... jamais	*never*
ne ... que	*only*
ne ... aucun(e)	*no*
ne ... nul(le)	*no*
ne ... nulle part	*nowhere*
ne ... ni	*neither ... nor*
ne ... ni ... ni	*neither ... nor*

◆ Word order

– In simple tenses and the imperative:
ne precedes the verb (and any object pronouns) and the second element follows the verb → ①

– In compound tenses:

i   **ne ... pas, ne ... point, ne ... rien, ne ... plus, ne ... jamais, ne... guère** follow the pattern:
     **ne + auxiliary verb + pas + past participle → ②

ii   **ne ... personne, ne ... que, ne ... aucun(e), ne ... nul(le), ne ... nulle part, ne ... ni (... ni)** follow the pattern:
    **ne + auxiliary verb + past participle + personne → ③

– With a verb in the infinitive:
ne ... pas, ne ... point (*etc* see i above) come together → ④

◆ For use of **rien**, **personne** and **aucun** as pronouns, see p 178.

1. **Je ne fume pas**
   I don't smoke
   Ne changez rien
   Don't change anything
   Je ne vois personne
   I can't see anybody
   Nous ne nous verrons plus
   We won't see each other any more
   Il n'arrive jamais à l'heure
   He never arrives on time
   Il n'avait qu'une valise
   He only had one suitcase
   Je n'ai reçu aucune réponse
   I have received no reply
   Il ne boit ni ne fume
   He neither drinks nor smokes
   Ni mon fils ni ma fille ne les connaissaient
   Neither my son nor my daughter knew them

2. **Elle n'a pas fait ses devoirs**
   She hasn't done her homework
   Ne vous a-t-il rien dit?
   Didn't he say anything to you?
   Ils n'avaient jamais vu une si belle maison
   They had never seen such a beautiful house
   Tu n'as guère changé
   You've hardly changed

3. **Je n'ai parlé à personne**
   I haven't spoken to anybody
   Il n'avait mangé que la moitié du repas
   He had only eaten half the meal
   Elle ne les a trouvés nulle part
   She couldn't find them anywhere
   Il ne l'avait ni vu ni entendu
   He had neither seen nor heard him

4. **Il essayait de ne pas rire**
   He was trying not to laugh

☐ **Negatives** *(Continued)*

◆ Combination of negatives. These are the most common combinations of negative particles:

ne ... plus jamais	→ 1
ne ... plus personne	→ 2
ne ... plus rien	→ 3
ne ... plus ni ... ni ...	→ 4
ne ... jamais personne	→ 5
ne ... jamais rien	→ 6
ne ... jamais que	→ 7
ne ... jamais ni ... ni ...	→ 8
(ne ... pas) non plus	→ 9

non and **pas**

◆ **non** *no* is the usual negative response to a question → 10
  It is often translated as *not* → 11

◆ **pas** is generally used when a distinction is being made, or for emphasis → 12
  It is often translated as *not* → 13

Grammar

1. **Je ne le ferai plus jamais**
   I'll never do it again

2. **Je ne connais plus personne à Rouen**
   I don't know anybody in Rouen any more

3. **Ces marchandises ne valaient plus rien**
   Those goods were no longer worth anything

4. **Ils n'ont plus ni chats ni chiens**
   They no longer have either cats or dogs

5. **On n'y voit jamais personne**
   You never see anybody there

6. **Ils ne font jamais rien d'intéressant**
   They never do anything interesting

7. **Je n'ai jamais parlé qu'à sa femme**
   I've only ever spoken to his wife

8. **Il ne m'a jamais ni écrit ni téléphoné**
   He has never either written to me or phoned me

9. **Ils n'ont pas d'enfants et nous non plus**
   They don't have any children and neither do we
   Je ne les aime pas – Moi non plus
   I don't like them – Neither do I/I don't either

10. **Vous voulez nous accompagner? – Non**
    Do you want to come with us? – No (I don't)

11. **Tu viens ou non?**
    Are you coming or not?
    J'espère que non
    I hope not

12. **Ma sœur aime le ski, moi pas**
    My sister likes skiing, I don't

13. **Qui a fait ça? – Pas moi!**
    Who did that? – Not me!
    Est-il de retour? – Pas encore
    Is he back? – Not yet
    Tu as froid? – Pas du tout
    Are you cold? – Not at all

❑ Question forms: direct

There are four ways of forming direct questions in French:

- by inverting the normal word order so that *pronoun subject + verb* → *verb + pronoun subject*. A hyphen links the verb and pronoun → ①

  - When the subject is a noun, a pronoun is inserted after the verb and linked to it by a hyphen → ②

  - When the verb ends in a vowel in the third person singular, **-t-** is inserted before the pronoun → ③

- by maintaining the word order *subject + verb*, but by using a rising intonation at the end of the sentence → ④

- by inserting **est-ce que** before the construction *subject + verb* → ⑤

- by using an interrogative word at the beginning of the sentence, together with inversion *or* the **est-ce que** form above → ⑥

1 | **Aimez-vous la France?** | **Avez-vous fini?**
Do you like France? | Have you finished?
Est-ce possible? | **Est-elle restée?**
Is it possible? | Did she stay?
Part-on tout de suite?
Are we leaving right away?

2 | **Tes parents sont-ils en vacances?**
Are your parents on holiday?
Jean-Benoît est-il parti?
Has Jean-Benoît left?

3 | **A-t-elle de l'argent?**
Has she any money?
La pièce dure-t-elle longtemps?
Does the play last long?
Mon père a-t-il téléphoné?
Has my father phoned?

4 | **Il l'a fini** | **Il l'a fini?**
He's finished it | Has he finished it?
Robert va venir | **Robert va venir?**
Robert's coming | Is Robert coming?

5 | **Est-ce que tu la connais?**
Do you know her?
Est-ce que tes parents sont revenus d'Italie?
Have your parents come back from Italy?

6 | **Quel train** { **prends-tu?**
                est-ce que tu prends?
What train are you getting?

     Lequel { **est-ce que ta sœur préfère?**
                 ta sœur préfère-t-elle?
Which one does your sister prefer?

     Quand { **êtes-vous arrivé?**
               est-ce que vous êtes arrivé?
When did you arrive?

     Pourquoi { **ne sont-ils pas venus?**
                   est-ce qu'ils ne sont pas venus?
Why haven't they come?

◻ Question forms: indirect

An indirect question is one that is 'reported', e.g. he asked me *what the time was*, tell me *which way to go*. Word order in indirect questions is as follows:

- *interrogative word* + subject + verb → ①

- when the subject is a noun, and not a pronoun, the subject and verb are often inverted → ②

◻ n'est-ce pas

This is used wherever English would use *isn't it?*, *don't they?*, *weren't we?*, *is it?* etc tagged on to the end of a sentence → ③

◻ oui and si

Oui is the word for *yes* in answer to a question put in the affirmative → ④

Si is the word for *yes* in answer to a question put in the negative or to contradict a negative statement → ⑤

1. **Je me demande s'il viendra**
   I wonder if he'll come
   Je ne sais pas à quoi ça sert
   I don't know what it's for
   Dites-moi quel autobus va à la gare
   Tell me which bus goes to the station
   Il m'a demandé combien d'argent j'avais
   He asked me how much money I had

2. **Elle ne sait pas à quelle heure commence le film**
   She doesn't know what time the film starts
   Je me demande où sont mes clés
   I wonder where my keys are
   Elle nous a demandé comment allait notre père
   She asked us how our father was
   Je ne sais pas ce que veulent dire ces mots
   I don't know what these words mean

3. **Il fait chaud, n'est-ce pas?**
   It's warm, isn't it?
   Vous n'oublierez pas, n'est-ce pas?
   You won't forget, will you?

4. **Tu l'as fait? – Oui**
   Have you done it? – Yes (I have)

5. **Tu ne l'as pas fait? – Si**
   Haven't you done it? – Yes (I have)

Cardinal		**Ordinal**	
(one, two etc)		*(first, second etc)*	
zéro	0		
un (une)	1	premier (première)	1er, 1ère
deux	2	deuxième, second(e)	2ème
trois	3	troisième	3ème
quatre	4	quatrième	4ème
cinq	5	cinquième	5ème
six	6	sixième	6ème
sept	7	septième	7ème
huit	8	huitième	8ème
neuf	9	neuvième	9ème
dix	10	dixième	10ème
onze	11	onzième	11ème
douze	12	douzième	12ème
treize	13	treizième	13ème
quatorze	14	quatorzième	14ème
quinze	15	quinzième	15ème
seize	16	seizième	16ème
dix-sept	17	dix-septième	17ème
dix-huit	18	dix-huitième	18ème
dix-neuf	19	dix-neuvième	19ème
vingt	20	vingtième	20ème
vingt et un (une)	21	vingt et unième	21ème
vingt-deux	22	vingt-deuxième	22ème
vingt-trois	23	vingt-troisième	23ème
trente	30	trentième	30ème
quarante	40	quarantième	40ème
cinquante	50	cinquantième	50ème
soixante	60	soixantième	60ème
soixante-dix	70	soixante-dixième	70ème
soixante et onze	71	soixante-onzième	71ème
soixante-douze	72	soixante-douzième	72ème
quatre-vingts	80	quatre-vingtième	80ème
quatre-vingt-un (une)	81	quatre-vingt-unième	81ème
quatre-vingt-dix	90	quatre-vingt-dixième	90ème
quatre-vingt-onze	91	quatre-vingt-onzième	91ème

```
4 6 2
8 1 5
9 3 1
```

Cardinal

cent	100
cent un (une)	101
cent deux	102
cent dix	110
cent quarante-deux	142
deux cents	200
deux cent un (une)	201
deux cent deux	202
trois cents	300
quatre cents	400
cinq cents	500
six cents	600
sept cents	700
huit cents	800
neuf cents	900
mille	1000
mille un (une)	1001
mille deux	1002
deux mille	2000
cent mille	100.000
un million	1.000.000
deux millions	2.000.000

Ordinal

centième	100ème
cent unième	101ème
cent deuxième	102ème
cent dixième	110ème
cent quarante-deuxième	142ème
deux centième	200ème
deux cent unième	201ème
deux cent-deuxième	202ème
trois centième	300ème
quatre centième	400ème
cinq centième	500ème
six centième	600ème
sept centième	700ème
huit centième	800ème
neuf centième	900ème
millième	1000ème
mille unième	1001ème
mille deuxième	1002ème
deux millième	2000ème
cent millième	100.000ème
millionième	1.000.000ème
deux millionième	2.000.000ème

Fractions

un demi, une demie	a half
un tiers	a third
deux tiers	two thirds
un quart	a quarter
trois quarts	three quarters
un cinquième	one fifth
cinq et trois quarts	
five and three quarters	

Others

zéro virgule cinq (0,5)	0.5
un virgule trois (1,3)	1.3
dix pour cent	10%
deux plus deux	2 + 2
deux moins deux	2 - 2
deux fois deux	2 x 2
deux divisé par deux	2 ÷ 2

⚠ NOTE the use of points with large numbers and commas with fractions, i.e. the opposite of English usage.

```
4 6 2
8 1 5
9 3 1
```

NUMBERS   226

◻ Other Uses

- **-aine** denoting approximate numbers:

une douzaine (de pommes)	about a dozen (apples)
une quinzaine (d'hommes)	about fifteen (men)
des centaines de personnes	hundreds of people
BUT: **un millier (de voitures)**	about a thousand (cars)

- measurements:

vingt mètres carrés	20 square metres
vingt mètres cubes	20 cubic metres
un pont long de quarante mètres	a bridge 40 metres long
avoir trois mètres de large/de haut	to be 3 metres wide/ high

- miscellaneous:

Il habite au dix	He lives at number 10
C'est au chapitre sept	It's in chapter 7
(C'est) à la page 17	(It's) on page 17
(Il habite) au septième étage	(He lives) on the 7th floor
Il est arrivé le septième	He came in 7th
échelle au vingt-cinq millième	scale 1:25,000

Telephone numbers

Je voudrais Édimbourg trois cent trente, vingt-deux, dix
I would like Edinburgh 330 2210

Je voudrais le soixante-cinq, treize, vingt-deux, zéro deux
Could you get me 65 13 22 02

Poste trois cent trente-cinq
Extension number 335

Poste vingt-deux, trente-trois
Extension number 2233

⚠ NOTE In French, telephone numbers are broken down into groups of two or three numbers (never four), and are not spoken separately as in English. They are also written in groups of two or three numbers.

◻ Dates

Quelle est la date d'aujourd'hui?	} What's the date today?
Quel jour sommes-nous?	

C'est ...	} It's the ...
Nous sommes ...	
le premier février	1st of February
le deux février	2nd of February
le vingt-huit février	28th of February
Il vient le sept mars	He's coming on the 7th of March

⚠ NOTE Use cardinal numbers except for the first of the month.

◻ Years

Je suis né en 1971	I was born in 1971

le douze février { **dix-neuf cent soixante et onze**
mil neuf cent soixante et onze
(on) 12th February 1971

⚠ NOTE There are two ways of expressing the year (see last example). Note the spelling of **mil** *one thousand* in dates.

◻ Other expressions

dans les années cinquante	during the fifties
au vingtième siècle	in the twentieth century
en mai	in May
lundi (quinze)	on Monday (the 15th)
le lundi	on Mondays
dans dix jours	in 10 days' time
il y a dix jours	10 days ago

Quelle heure est-il?	*What time is it?*
Il est …	*It's …*

00.00	**minuit** *midnight, twelve o'clock*
00.10	**minuit dix, zéro heure dix**
00.15	**minuit et quart, zéro heure quinze**
00.30	**minuit et demi, zéro heure trente**
00.45	**une heure moins (le) quart, zéro heure quarante-cinq**

01.00	**une heure du matin** *one a.m., one o'clock in the morning*
01.10	**une heure dix (du matin)**
01.15	**une heure et quart, une heure quinze**
01.30	**une heure et demie, une heure trente**
01.45	**deux heures moins (le) quart, une heure quarante-cinq**
01.50	**deux heures moins dix, une heure cinquante**
01.59	**deux heures moins une, une heure cinquante-neuf**

12.00	**midi, douze heures** *noon, twelve o'clock*
12.30	**midi et demi, douze heures trente**

13.00	**une heure de l'après-midi, treize heures** *one p.m., one o'clock in the afternoon*
01.30	**une heure et demie (de l'après-midi), treize heures trente**

19.00	**sept heures du soir, dix-neuf heures** *seven p.m., seven o'clock in the evening*
19.30	**sept heures et demie (du soir), dix-neuf heures trente**

À quelle heure venez-vous? – À sept heures
What time are you coming? – At seven o'clock
Les bureaux sont fermés de midi à quatorze heures
The offices are closed from twelve until two
à deux heures du matin/de l'après-midi
at two o'clock in the morning/afternoon, at two a.m./p.m.
à sept heures du soir
at seven o'clock in the evening, at seven p.m.
à cinq heures précises *or* **pile**
at five o'clock sharp
vers neuf heures
about nine o'clock
peu avant/après midi
shortly before/after noon
entre huit et neuf heures
between eight and nine o'clock
Il est plus de trois heures et demie
It's after half past three
Il faut y être à dix heures au plus tard/au plus tôt
You have to be there by ten o'clock at the latest/earliest
Ne venez pas plus tard que onze heures moins le quart
Come no later than a quarter to eleven
Il en a pour une demi-heure
He'll be half an hour (at it)
Elle est restée sans connaissance pendant un quart d'heure
She was unconscious for a quarter of an hour
Je les attends depuis une heure
I've been waiting for them for an hour/since one o'clock
Ils sont partis il y a quelques minutes
They left a few minutes ago
Je l'ai fait en vingt minutes
I did it in twenty minutes
Le train arrive dans une heure
The train arrives in an hour('s time)
Combien de temps dure ce film?
How long does this film last?

Beware of translating word for word. While on occasion this is quite possible, quite often it is not. The need for caution is illustrated by the following:

- English phrasal verbs (i.e. verbs followed by a preposition) e.g. *to run away*, *to fall down* are often translated by one word in French → 1

- English verbal constructions often contain a preposition where none exists in French, or vice versa → 2

- Two or more prepositions in English may have a single rendering in French → 3

- A word which is singular in English may be plural in French, or vice versa → 4

- French has no equivalent of the possessive construction denoted by *--'s/--s'* → 5

See also *at/in/to*, p 234.

Specific problems
-ing

This is translated in a variety of ways in French:

- *to be …-ing* is translated by a simple verb → 6
  EXCEPTION: when a physical position is denoted, a past participle is used → 7

- in the construction *to see/hear sb …-ing*, use an infinitive or **qui** + verb → 8

-ing can also be translated by:
  – an infinitive → 9 (see p 44)
  – a perfect infinitive → 10 (see p 46)
  – a present participle → 11 (see p 48)
  – a noun → 12

Examples

Grammar

1	**s'enfuir** to run away	**tomber** to fall down	**céder** to give in
2	**payer** to pay for	**regarder** to look at	**écouter** to listen to
	obéir à to obey	**nuire à** to harm	**manquer de** to lack
3	**s'étonner de** to be surprised at	**satisfait de** satisfied with	
	voler qch à to steal sth from	**apte à** capable of; fit for	
4	**les bagages** the luggage	**ses cheveux** his/her hair	
	le bétail the cattle	**mon pantalon** my trousers	
5	**la voiture de mon frère** my brother's car *(literally: … of my brother)*	**la chambre des enfants** the children's bedroom *(literally: … of the children)*	
6	**Il part demain** He's leaving tomorrow	**Je lisais un roman** I was reading a novel	
7	**Elle est assise là-bas** She's sitting over there	**Il était couché par terre** He was lying on the ground	

8 **Je les vois** { **venir** / **qui viennent** } I can see them coming

Je l'ai entendue { **chanter** / **qui chantait** } I heard her singing

9	**J'aime aller au cinéma** I like going to the cinema	**Arrêtez de parler!** Stop talking!
	Au lieu de répondre Instead of answering	**Avant de partir** Before leaving

10 **Après avoir ouvert la boîte, il …**
After opening the box, he …

11 **Étant plus timide que moi, elle …**
Being shyer than me, she …

12 **Le ski me maintient en forme**
Skiing keeps me fit

to be

- Generally translated by **être** → ①
  When physical location is implied, **se trouver** may be used → ②

- In set expressions, describing physical and emotional conditions, **avoir** is used:

avoir chaud/froid	to be warm/cold
avoir faim/soif	to be hungry/thirsty
avoir peur/honte	to be afraid/ashamed
avoir tort/raison	to be wrong/right

- Describing the weather, e.g. *what's the weather like?*, *it's windy/sunny*, use **faire** → ③

- For ages, e.g. *he is 6*, use **avoir** → ④

- For state of health, e.g. *he's unwell, how are you?*, use **aller** → ⑤

it is, it's

- Usually **il/elle est**, when referring to a noun → ⑥

- For expressions of time, also use **il est** → ⑦

- To describe the weather, e.g. *it's windy*, see above.

- In the construction: *it is difficult/easy to do sth*, use **il est** → ⑧

- In all other constructions, use **c'est** → ⑨

there is/there are

- Both are translated by **il y a** → ⑩

can, be able

- Physical ability is expressed by **pouvoir** → ⑪

- If the meaning is *to know how to*, use **savoir** → ⑫

- *Can* + a 'verb of hearing or seeing *etc*' in English is not translated in French → ⑬

1. **Il est tard**   **C'est peu probable**
   It's late   It's not very likely

2. **Où se trouve la gare?**
   Where's the station?

3. **Quel temps fait-il?**   **Il fait beau/mauvais/du vent**
   What's the weather like?   It's lovely/miserable/windy

4. **Quel âge avez-vous?**   **J'ai quinze ans**
   How old are you?   I'm fifteen

5. **Comment allez-vous?**   **Je vais très bien**
   How are you?   I'm very well

6. **Où est mon parapluie? – Il est là, dans le coin**
   Where's my umbrella? – It's there, in the corner
   Descends la valise si elle n'est pas trop lourde
   Bring down the case if it isn't too heavy

7. **Quelle heure est-il? – Il est sept heures et demie**
   What's the time? – It's half past seven

8. **Il est difficile de répondre à cette question**
   It's difficult to reply to this question

9. **C'est moi qui ne l'aime pas**
   It's me who doesn't like him
   C'est Charles/ma mère qui l'a dit
   It's Charles/my mother who said so
   C'est ici que je les ai achetés
   It's here that I bought them
   C'est parce que la poste est fermée que …
   It's because the post office is closed that …

10. **Il y a quelqu'un à la porte**
    There's somebody at the door
    Il y a cinq livres sur la table
    There are five books on the table

11. **Pouvez-vous atteindre cette étagère?**
    Can you reach up to that shelf?

12. **Elle ne sait pas nager**
    She can't swim

13. **Je ne vois rien**   **Il les entendait**
    I can't see anything   He could hear them

to (see also below)

• Generally translated by **à** → ①
  (See p 204).

• In time expressions, e.g. *10 to 6*, use **moins** → ②

• When the meaning is *in order to*, use **pour** → ③

• Following a verb, as in *to try to do, to like to do*, see pp 44 and 64

• *easy/difficult/impossible etc to do*:
  The preposition used depends on whether a specific noun is referred
  to → ④ or not → ⑤

at/in/to

• With feminine countries, use **en** → ⑥
  With masculine countries, use **au** (**aux** with plural countries) → ⑦

• With towns, use **à** → ⑧

• *at/to the butcher's/grocer's etc*: use **à** + noun designating the
  shop, or **chez** + noun designating the shopkeeper → ⑨

• *at/to the dentist's/doctor's etc*: use **chez** → ⑩

• *at/to ...'s/...s' house*: use **chez** → ⑪

Grammar

1. **Donne le livre à Patrick**
   Give the book to Patrick

2. **dix heures moins cinq**   **à sept heures moins le quart**
   five to ten   at a quarter to seven

3. **Je l'ai fait pour vous aider**
   I did it to help you
   Il se pencha pour nouer son lacet
   He bent down to tie his shoelace

4. **Ce livre est difficile à lire**
   This book is difficult to read

5. **Il est difficile de comprendre leurs raisons**
   It's difficult to understand their reasons

6. **Il est allé en France/en Suisse**
   He has gone to France/to Switzerland
   un village en Norvège/en Belgique
   a village in Norway/in Belgium

7. **Êtes-vous allé au Canada/au Danemark/aux États-Unis?**
   Have you been to Canada/to Denmark/to the United States?
   une ville au Japon/au Brésil
   a town in Japan/in Brazil

8. **Il est allé à Vienne/à Bruxelles**
   He has gone to Vienna/to Brussels
   Il habite à Londres/à Genève
   He lives in London/in Geneva
   Ils logent dans un hôtel à St. Pierre
   They're staying in a hotel at St. Pierre

9. **Je l'ai acheté** { **à l'épicerie**   I bought it at the grocer's
               { **chez l'épicier**
   Elle est allée { **à la boulangerie**   She's gone to the baker's
                { **chez le boulanger**

10. **J'ai un rendez-vous chez le dentiste**
    I've an appointment at the dentist's
    Il est allé chez le médecin
    He has gone to the doctor's

11. **chez Christian**   **chez les Pagot**
    at/to Christian's house   at/to the Pagots' house

❐ General Points

◆ Activity of the lips

The lips play a very important part in French. When a vowel is described as having 'rounded' lips, the lips are slightly drawn together and pursed, as when an English speaker expresses exaggerated surprise with the vowel 'ooh!' Equally, if the lips are said to be 'spread', the corners are pulled firmly back towards the cheeks, tending to reveal the front teeth.

In English, lip position is not important, and vowel sounds tend to merge because of this. In French, the activity of the lips means that every vowel sound is clearly distinct from every other.

◆ No diphthongs

A diphthong is a glide between two vowel sounds in the same syllable. In English, there are few 'pure' vowel sounds, but largely diphthongs instead. Although speakers of English may *think they* produce one vowel sound in the word 'day', in fact they use a diphthong, which in this instance is a glide between the vowels [e] and [ɪ]: [deɪ]. In French the tension maintained in the lips, tongue and the mouth in general prevents diphthongs occurring, as the vowel sound is kept constant throughout. Hence the French word corresponding to the above example, 'dé', is pronounced with no final [ɪ] sound, but is phonetically represented thus: [de].

◆ Consonants

In English, consonants are often pronounced with a degree of laxness that can result in their practically disappearing altogether although not strictly 'silent'. In a relaxed pronunciation of a word such as 'hat', the 't' is often scarcely heard, or is replaced by a 'glottal stop' (a sort of jerk in the throat). This never occurs in French, where consonants are always given their full value.

◻ Pronunciation of Consonants

Some consonants are pronounced almost exactly as in English: [b, p, f, v, g, k, m, w].

Most others are similar to English, but slight differences should be noted.

EXAMPLES	HINTS ON PRONUNCIATION
[d] **d**inde	
[t] **t**ente	The tip of the tongue touches the upper front teeth and not the roof of the mouth as in English
[n] **n**onne	
[l] Li**ll**e	
[s] tou**s ç**a	The tip of the tongue is down behind the bottom front teeth, lower than in English
[z] **z**éro ro**s**e	
[ʃ] **ch**ose ta**ch**e	Like the *sh* of English *shout*
[ʒ] **j**e **g**ilet bei**g**e	Like the *s* of English *measure*
[j] **y**eux pai**ll**e	Like the *y* of English *yes*

Three consonants are not heard in English:

[ʀ] **r**a**r**e veni**r**	R is often silent in English, e.g. fa*r*m. In French the [ʀ] is never silent, unless it follows an **e** at the end of a word e.g. cherch**er**. To pronounce it, try to make a short sound like gargling. Similar, too, to the Scottish pronunciation of *loch*
[ɲ] vi**gn**e a**gn**eau	Similar to the *ni* of Spa*ni*ard
[ɥ] **h**uile l**u**eur	Like a very rapid [y] (see p 239) followed immediately by the next vowel of the word

◻ Pronunciation of Vowels

	EXAMPLES	HINTS ON PRONUNCIATION
[a]	patte plat amour	Similar to the vowel in English *pat*
[ɑ]	bas pâte	Longer than the sound above, it resembles the English exclamation of surprise *ah!* Similar, too, to the English vowel in *car* without the final *r* sound
[ɛ]	lait jouet merci	Similar to the English vowel in *pet*. Beware of using the English diphthong [eɪ] as in *pay*
[e]	été jouer	A pure vowel, again quite different from the diphthong in English *pay*
[ə]	le premier	Similar to the English sound in *butter* when the *r* is not pronounced
[i]	ici vie lycee	The lips are well spread towards the cheeks while uttering this sound. Shorter than the English vowel in *see*
[ɔ]	mort homme	The lips are well rounded while producing a sound similar to the *o* of English *cot*
[o]	mot dôme eau	A pure vowel with strongly rounded lips quite different from the diphthong in English *bone, low*

[u] gen**ou** r**ou**e	A pure vowel with strongly rounded lips. Similar to the English *ooh!* of surprise
[y] r**ue** v**ê**tu	Often the most difficult for English speakers to produce: round your lips and try to pronounce [i] (see above). There is no [j] sound (see p 237) as there is in English *pure*
[œ] s**œu**r b**eu**rre	Similar to the vowel in English *fir* or *murmur*, but without the *r* sound and with the lips more strongly rounded
[ø] p**eu** d**eu**x	To pronounce this, try to say [e] (see above) with the lips strongly rounded

Nasal Vowels

These are spelt with a vowel followed by a 'nasal' consonant – **n** or **m**. The production of nasal vowels really requires the help of a teacher or a recording of the sound. However, to help you, the vowel is pronounced by allowing the air from the lungs to come partly down the nose and partly through the mouth, and the **n** or **m** is not pronounced at all.

[ɑ̃] l**en**t s**an**g d**an**s	In each case, the vowel shown in the phonetic symbol is pronounced as described above, but air is allowed to come through the nose as well as the mouth
[ɛ̃] mat**in** pl**ein**	
[ɔ̃] n**on** p**on**t	
[œ̃] br**un** **un** parf**um**	

▢ From Spelling to Sounds

Although it may not seem so at first sight, there are some fairly precise 'rules' which can help you to know how to pronounce French words from their spelling.

Vowels

SPELLING	PRONOUNCED	EXAMPLES
a, à	[a]	chatte, table
a, â	[ɑ]	pâte, pas
e, é	[e]	été, marcher
e, é, ê	[ɛ]	fenêtre, fermer, chère
e	[ə]	double, fenêtre
i, î, y	[i]	lit, abîmer, lycée
o, ô	[o]	pot, trop, dôme
o	[ɔ]	sotte, orange
u, û	[y]	battu, fût, pur

Vowel Groups

There are several groups of vowels in French spelling which are regularly pronounced in the same way:

ai	[ɛ] or [e]	maison, marchai, faire
ail	[aj]	portail
ain, aim, (c)in, im	[ɛ̃]	pain, faim, frein, impair
au	[o]	auberge, landau
an, am, en, em	[ɑ̃]	plan, ample, entrer, temps
eau	[o]	bateau, eau
eu	[œ] or [ø]	feu, peur
euil(le), ueil	[œj]	feuille, recueil
oi, oy	[wa]	voire, voyage
on, om	[ɔ̃]	ton, compter
ou	[u]	hibou, outil
œu	[œ]	sœur, cœur
ue	[y]	rue
un, um	[œ̃]	brun, parfum

Added to these are the many groups of letters occurring at the end of words, where their pronunciation is predictable, bearing in mind the tendency (see p 242) of final consonants to remain silent:

TYPICAL WORDS	PRONUNCIATION OF FINAL SYLLABLE
pas, mât, chat	[ɑ] or [a]
marcher, marchez, marchais, marchait, baie, valet, mes, fumée	[e] or [ɛ]
nid	[i]
chaud, vaut, faux, sot, tôt, Pernod, dos, croc	[o]
bout, bijoux, sous, boue	[u]
fut, fût, crus, crûs	[y]
queue, heureux, bleus	[ø]
en, vend, vent, an, sang, grand, dans	[ɑ̃]
fin, feint, frein, vain	[ɛ̃]
on, pont, fond, avons	[ɔ̃]
brun, parfum	[œ̃]

□ **From Spelling to Sounds** *(Continued)*

Consonants

- Final consonants are usually silent → ☐1

- **n** or **m** at the end of a syllable or word are silent, but they have the effect of 'nasalizing' the preceding vowel(s) (see p 239 on Nasal Vowels)

- The letter **h** is either 'silent' ('mute') or 'aspirate' when it begins a word. When silent, the word behaves as though it started with a vowel and takes a liaison with the preceding word where appropriate.

  When the **h** is aspirate, no liaison is made → ☐2

  There is no way of predicting which words start with which sort of **h** – this simply has to be learnt with each word

- The following consonants in spelling have predictable pronunciations: b, d, f, k, l, p, r, t, v, w, x, y, z. Others vary:

SPELLING	PRONOUNCED	ENGLISH EXAMPLES	
c + a, o, u	[k]	**c**an, **c**ot, **c**ut	→ ☐3
+ l, r		**cl**ass, **cr**am	
c + e, i, y	[s]	**c**eiling, i**c**e	→ ☐4
ç + a, o, u	[s]	**c**eiling, i**c**e	→ ☐5
ch	[ʃ]	**sh**op, la**sh**	→ ☐6
g + a, o, u	[g]	**g**ate, **g**ot, **g**un	→ ☐7
+ l, r		**gl**ass, **gr**amme	
g + e, i, y	[ʒ]	lei**s**ure	→ ☐8
gn	[ɲ]	compa**ni**on, o**ni**on	→ ☐9
j	[ʒ]	mea**s**ure	→ ☐10
q, qu	[k]	**q**uay, **k**it	→ ☐11
s between vowels	[z]	ro**s**e	→ ☐12
elsewhere	[s]	**s**it	
th	[t]	**Th**omas	→ ☐13
t in **-tion**	[s]	**s**it	→ ☐14

1	**éclat**	**nez**	
	[ekla]	[ne]	
	chaud	**aider**	
	[ʃo]	[ɛde]	
2	silent **h**:	aspirate **h**:	
	des hôtels	**des haricots**	
	[de zotɛl]	[de aʀiko]	
3	**café**	**côte**	**culture**
	[kafe]	[kot]	[kyltyʀ]
	classe	**croûte**	
	[klas]	[kʀut]	
4	**ceci**	**cil**	**cycliste**
	[səsi]	[sil]	[siklist]
5	**ça**	**garçon**	**déçu**
	[sa]	[gaʀsɔ̃]	[desy]
6	**chat**	**riche**	
	[ʃa]	[ʀiʃ]	
7	**gare**	**gourde**	**aigu**
	[gaʀ]	[guʀd]	[egy]
	glaise	**gramme**	
	[glɛz]	[gʀam]	
8	**gemme**	**gilet**	**gymnaste**
	[ʒem]	[ʒilɛ]	[ʒimnast]
9	**vigne**	**oignon**	
	[viɲ]	[ɔɲɔ̃]	
10	**joli**	**Jules**	
	[ʒɔli]	[ʒyl]	
11	**quiche**	**quitter**	
	[kiʃ]	[kite]	
12	**sable**	**maison**	
	[sablə]	[mɛzɔ̃]	
13	**théâtre**	**Thomas**	
	[teatʀ]	[tɔma]	
14	**nation**	**action**	
	[nasjɔ̃]	[aksjɔ̃]	

◻ Feminine Forms and Pronunciation

- For adjectives and nouns ending in a vowel in the masculine, the addition of an **e** to form the feminine does not alter the pronunciation → 1

- If the masculine ends with a silent consonant, generally **-d**, **-s**, **-r** or **-t**, the consonant is sounded in the feminine → 2
  This also applies when the final consonant is doubled before the addition of the feminine **e** → 3

- If the masculine ends in a nasal vowel and a silent **n**, e.g. **-an**, **-on**, **-in**, the vowel is no longer nasalized and the **-n** is pronounced in the feminine → 4
  This also applies when the final **-n** is doubled before the addition of the feminine **e** → 5

- Where the masculine and feminine forms have totally different endings (see pp 136 and 150), the pronunciation of course varies accordingly → 6

◻ Plural Forms and Pronunciation

- The addition of **s** or **x** to form regular plurals generally does not affect pronunciation → 7

- Where liaison has to be made, the final **-s** or **-x** of the plural form is pronounced → 8

- Where the masculine singular and plural forms have totally different endings (see pp 138 and 148), the pronunciation of course varies accordingly → 9

- Note the change in pronunciation in the following nouns:

SINGULAR		PLURAL		
bœuf	[bœf]	**bœufs**	[bø]	ox/oxen
œuf	[œf]	**œufs**	[ø]	egg/eggs
os	[ɔs]	**os**	[o]	bone/bones

	ADJECTIVES		NOUNS	
1	**joli** [ʒɔli]	→ **jolie** [ʒɔli]	**un ami** [ami]	→ **une amie** [ami]
	déçu [desy]	→ **déçue** [desy]	**un employé** [ãplwaje]	→ **une employée** [ãplwaje]
2	**chaud** [ʃo]	→ **chaude** [ʃod]	**un étudiant** [etydjã]	→ **une étudiante** [etydjãt]
	français [frãsɛ]	→ **française** [frãsɛz]	**un Anglais** [ãglɛ]	→ **une Anglaise** [ãglɛz]
	inquiet [ɛ̃kjɛ]	→ **inquiète** [ɛ̃kjɛt]	**un étranger** [etrãʒe]	→ **une étrangère** [etrãʒɛr]
3	**violet** [vjɔlɛ]	→ **violette** [vjɔlɛt]	**le cadet** [kadɛ]	→ **la cadette** [kadɛt]
	gras [gra]	→ **grasse** [gras]		
4	**plein** [plɛ̃]	→ **pleine** [plɛn]	**le souverain** [suvrɛ̃]	→ **la souveraine** [suvrɛn]
	fin [fɛ̃]	→ **fine** [fin]	**Le Persan** [pɛrsã]	→ **la Persane** [pɛrsan]
	brun [brœ̃]	→ **brune** [bryn]	**le voisin** [vwazɛ̃]	→ **la voisine** [vwazin]
5	**canadien** [kanadjɛ̃]	→ **canadienne** [kanadjɛn]	**le paysan** [pɛizã]	→ **la paysanne** [pɛizan]
	breton [brətɔ̃]	→ **bretonne** [brətɔn]	**le baron** [barɔ̃]	→ **la baronne** [barɔn]
6	**vif** [vif]	→ **vive** [viv]	**le veuf** [vœf]	→ **la veuve** [vœv]
	traître [trɛtrə]	→ **traîtresse** [trɛtrɛs]	**le maître** [mɛtrə]	→ **la maîtresse** [mɛtrɛs]
7	**beau** [bo]	→ **beaux** [bo]	**la maison** [mɛzɔ̃]	→ **les maisons** [mɛzɔ̃]
8	**des anciens élèves** [de zãsjɛ̃ zelɛv]		**de beaux arbres** [də bo zarbr(ə)]	
9	**amical** [amikal]	→ **amicaux** [amiko]	**un journal** [ʒurnal]	→ **des journaux** [ʒurno]

◻ The Alphabet

A, a	[ɑ]	**J, j**	[ʒi]	**S, s**	[ɛs]
B, b	[be]	**K, k**	[ka]	**T, t**	[te]
C, c	[se]	**L, l**	[ɛl]	**U, u**	[y]
D, d	[de]	**M, m**	[ɛm]	**V, v**	[ve]
E, e	[ə]	**N, n**	[ɛn]	**W,w**	[dubləve]
F, f	[ɛf]	**O, o**	[o]	**X, x**	[iks]
G, g	[ʒe]	**P, p**	[pe]	**Y, y**	[igʀɛk]
H, h	[aʃ]	**Q, q**	[ky]	**Z, z**	[zɛd]
I, i	[i]	**R, r**	[ɛʀ]		

Capital letters are used as in English except for the following:

- adjectives of nationality
  e.g. **une ville espagnole** **un auteur français**
  a Spanish town a French author

- languages
  e.g. **Parlez-vous anglais?** **Il parle français et allemand**
  Do you speak English? He speaks French and German

- days of the week:
lundi	Monday
mardi	Tuesday
mercredi	Wednesday
jeudi	Thursday
vendredi	Friday
samedi	Saturday
dimanche	Sunday

- months of the year:
janvier	January	**juillet**	July
février	February	**août**	August
mars	March	**septembre**	September
avril	April	**octobre**	October
mai	May	**novembre**	November
juin	June	**décembre**	December

The following index lists comprehensively both grammatical terms and key words in French and English contained in this book.